The
Cottagecore Baking Book

60 Sweet and Savory Bakes
for Simple, Cozy Living

Kayla Lobermeier

Creator of Under A Tin Roof™
and author of *The Prairie Kitchen Cookbook*

PAGE STREET
PUBLISHING CO.

To my children, you are my endless supply of creative inspiration. Thank you for being my favorite taste testers and my biggest cheerleaders. You are so loved, and I am honored to be your mama. Hugs and kisses.

To my family, without whom I would not be able to follow my passions. You are my foundation, the people who believe in me and continue to push me to reach for the dreams that I never thought could be possible.

To our Under A Tin Roof™ readers, I am so thankful to be able to share another book with you. Without your support, none of this would be possible! I hope that this book leaves you inspired to bake lots and lots of delicious baked goods in your cottages.

Contents

Introduction

Have you ever dreamed of living in a little thatched cottage surrounded by flowers? Do you love beautiful floral china and embroidered napkins? Do you find that the best medicine is spending an afternoon reading a romantic, historical fiction novel, sipping on a cup of herbal tea, and baking a sponge cake dressed with freshly picked fruit? If you love all of the aspects of living a slower-paced lifestyle that idealizes cottage living, then you will absolutely adore this cookbook!

During my childhood, I spent a majority of my time imagining that I lived in a past life, one that was filled with billowing skirts and linen aprons, tea parties and dainty fairy cakes, woodland animals and hidden magical gardens. I found solace in old-fashioned hobbies. Things like sewing, baking, and gardening felt like an extension of my personality that was altogether romantic, whimsical, and a little bit quirky. My friends and family would refer to me as an "old soul," though I would simply call myself a Connoisseur of Nostalgia.

With many of these ideals making up a larger part of the feminine aesthetic, there was no shortage of female empowerment in my childhood home. As a young girl, my dream was to write fantasy novels and create movies with pirate princesses as the leads. In fact, all of these aspects were what forged a path for my independence and confidence to begin a career as a Cottagecore content creator. My personal aesthetic has evolved over time. I have been many things: a single parent, a farmer and homesteader, a photographer and filmmaker, a writer, an artist, a recipe developer . . . to name a few! But one thing that has remained with me throughout my creative journey has been a love of enchanted cottage living intertwined with modern life.

If you are new to the Cottagecore phenomenon, then allow me to fill you in. This genre of internet content (images, videos, mood boards, cloth-ing lines, books, songs, and everything under the sun) began as a way for those of us who romanticize living in a bucolic fairytale to incorporate those nature-inspired and slow-living aspects into our everyday lives. In fact, this movement is nothing new. The concept of escaping into fairytale nostalgia has been around for centuries. It is a place where one can feel safe, calm, and at peace in a world that is so fast-paced and loud. This lovely aesthetic has forged the pathway for other aesthetics, like Fairycore and Grandmacore, to introduce themselves, and people from all walks of life are allowed to enjoy the softness and sentimentality that Cottagecore introduces. **Cottagecore is for everyone, anyone that wishes to live a softer, simpler life.**

With this book, my wish is to inspire you to bring yet another piece of the cottage into your life! Inside you will find recipes that are inspired by whimsy and fantasy along with coziness and feelings of visiting the countryside. English- and French-style baking influenced several recipes within these pages, and there are hints of vintage decorations and some rustic influences at every turn. Both sweet and savory bakes make an appearance, fashioned after the baked goods you might find in a pâtisserie from the illustrations in your favorite children's book. This baking book is full of wonderfully decorated desserts, but it will also help you learn the skills to create bakery-worthy confections in the comfort of your own home!

While we must live in a modern world, and for that I am personally very grateful, we can always enjoy a little taste of the cottage life by incorporating its elements into our routines. This all begins with little changes. Things like putting on a linen vest or tying ribbons in your hair, carrying a woven basket to the market, starting a backyard or container garden, knitting a scarf, or baking a pie are wonderful elements to add into your routine to embrace what slows things down and makes life so beautiful.

Come, sit down, and flip through these pages with your little floral teacup in hand and a fresh bouquet of wildflowers on the table. I hope that you find a tasty treat inside that makes you feel as if you have stepped into the cozy fantasy of your dreams.

xoxo

Kayla Lobermeier

Afternoon Tea Quick Breads, Muffins, and Scones

Time for a spot of tea. Won't you join me?

In the charming Victorian era, taking a leisurely pause for tea in the afternoon was incredibly popular. This tranquil break in the day between the early noon meal and a late, lengthy supper is often credited to the seventh Duchess of Bedford, Anna Maria Russell. This was sometime around 1840 and it eventually became a fond moment of the day for Queen Victoria. This was the perfect moment to indulge in delectable pastries and other delightful sweets.

As for my own afternoon tea, I adore serving a little sweet or savory baked good, especially when unexpected company pops in for a visit. These quick breads, muffins, and scones make for excellent, easy treats when time is scarce! They are a perfect complement to coffee or tea.

In this chapter, you will find recipes like Sweetheart Chocolate Chunk Scones (page 16), Hummingbird Bread with Cream Cheese Frosting (page 15), and Pecan Coffee Cake Muffins (page 11). For something more savory, give the Bacon, Cheddar, and Herb King Cornmeal Muffins (page 24) or Sweet Potato Sage Biscuits (page 20) a try. Each are wonderful for that little break in the day when we are craving something between meals.

Pecan Coffee Cake Muffins

Isn't coffee cake just the quintessential autumn treat for cozy afternoons? It's the perfect sweet to provide a feeling of comfort and warmth. Instead of baking a large cake, this recipe transforms a classic recipe into charming, individual muffins that can be packed up in a beautiful woven basket lined with a dainty napkin and taken on a journey to a friend's homey cottage. The combination of spicy autumnal flavors, crumbly streusel topping, and pecans transports you to a picturesque, small town with vibrant fall foliage, gentle breezes, and a cup of coffee in hand.

Preheat the oven to 425°F (218°C). Line a standard muffin pan with cupcake liners or grease and lightly flour the muffin cups. Set this aside while you make the muffins.

Begin by making the Pecan Crumble Topping. In a medium bowl, whisk together the flour, granulated sugar, brown sugar, cinnamon, and salt. Stir in the chopped pecans. Slowly drizzle in the melted butter, stirring while it is being added to the dry ingredients. Without overworking the crumble, stir until the butter is just soaked in and the flour is no longer dry, 1 to 2 minutes. The crumble should be coarse and clumpy, about the size of a pea. Cover the bowl with plastic wrap and place it in the freezer for about 20 minutes.

While the crumble is chilling, make the Pecan Coffee Cake Muffin batter. In a medium bowl, whisk together the flour, baking powder, cinnamon, baking soda, and salt. Set this aside.

In a large bowl, beat the butter and sugar together until it becomes light and fluffy, 3 to 4 minutes. Beat in the egg, egg white, and vanilla. In a glass measuring cup, whisk together the buttermilk and sour cream. Alternately, begin to add the flour mixture and the buttermilk mixture, beginning and ending with the flour mixture. With a wooden spoon or spatula, fold in the chopped pecans.

Fill each of the prepared muffin cups with batter about three-quarters of the way full. Remove the crumble topping from the freezer and sprinkle the tops of the muffins with the crumble. Bake the muffins for 10 to 12 minutes. Then, lower the oven temperature to 375°F (191°C) and bake the muffins for another 5 minutes, or until a toothpick inserted in the center comes out clean.

Let the muffins rest in their tin for about 10 minutes. Move the muffins to a wire cooling rack to finish cooling.

To make the Powdered Sugar Icing, whisk together the powdered sugar and milk until it is smooth and a bit runny. Drizzle the icing over the warm muffins before serving. To store the muffins, keep them in an airtight container at room temperature for about 5 days.

Makes about 12 muffins

Pecan Crumble Topping

¾ cup (94 g) all-purpose flour

3 tbsp (45 g) granulated sugar

3 tbsp (36 g) light brown sugar, packed

½ tsp ground cinnamon

¼ tsp kosher salt

¼ cup (25 g) finely chopped pecans

¼ cup (60 ml) melted salted butter, cooled slightly

Pecan Coffee Cake Muffins

1½ cups (188 g) all-purpose flour

3 tsp (14 g) baking powder

1 tsp ground cinnamon

½ tsp baking soda

¼ tsp kosher salt

½ cup (116 g) salted butter, softened

½ cup (100 g) granulated sugar

1 large egg

1 egg white

½ tsp vanilla extract

¼ cup (60 ml) buttermilk, room temperature

1 cup (240 ml) sour cream

1 cup (100 g) finely chopped pecans

Powdered Sugar Icing

1 cup (118 g) powdered sugar

2 tsp (10 ml) whole milk

Blackberry Ricotta Shortcakes

Did you know that a shortcake is really just a biscuit? These biscuits are made even dreamier with the addition of heavy cream in the dough, making them light, fluffy, and super soft. A shortcake is the perfect light dessert to enjoy on a hot summer's day. You will want to wander out to the back garden with a linen table cloth and your prettiest dishes to enjoy a few tantalizing bites. This dessert is more commonly served with strawberries, but you can make shortcakes with any of your favorite berries or fruits. After a day of picking blackberries, it will be the perfect time to bake up a batch of shortcakes with whipped ricotta cheese!

Preheat the oven to 425° F (218° F) and set aside a large, ungreased baking sheet.

To make the Macerated Blackberries, rinse the blackberries thoroughly. In a medium bowl, stir together the blackberries and the sugar. Cover the bowl with plastic wrap and let the berries rest on the countertop for at least 30 minutes to macerate. If you would like to speed up the process, you can cut the berries in half or into slices. Stir the berries occasionally.

While the berries are resting, make the Shortcake Biscuits. In a large bowl, whisk together the flour, baking powder, baking soda, and salt. Cut in the cold butter with a pastry blender or fork until the mixture resembles coarse crumbs about the size of a pea.

Stir in the buttermilk and heavy cream with a wooden spoon or silicone spatula. Bring the dough together with your hands until it is no longer dry and crumbly, about 2 minutes. On a lightly floured surface, fold the dough over itself about seven times to create layers in the dough.

Roll the dough out to about ½ inch (1.3 cm) thick and cut out the biscuits with a 3-inch (8-cm) round biscuit cutter. Be sure to cut straight down through the dough and do not twist the biscuit cutter. Alternately, you can cut the biscuits into shapes like diamonds or squares with a sharp knife, if you prefer something different!

Place the cut biscuits on the baking sheet about 2 inches (5 cm) apart. Brush them with a bit of extra heavy cream and sprinkle the tops with the coarse sugar. Before baking, chill the biscuits for about 30 minutes.

Bake the shortcakes for 20 to 22 minutes, or until they are golden brown on top and are no longer doughy in the middle. Let the biscuits rest for 5 to 10 minutes before slicing in half lengthwise.

Makes about 8 cakes

Macerated Blackberries

12 oz (336 g) fresh blackberries

½ cup (100 g) granulated sugar

Shortcake Biscuits

2¼ cups (281 g) all-purpose flour

2 tsp (9 g) baking powder

½ tsp baking soda

½ tsp kosher salt

½ cup (116 g) salted butter, cold and cut into ½-inch (1.3-cm) cubes

½ cup (120 ml) cold buttermilk

½ cup (120 ml) cold heavy cream, plus more for brushing

2 tbsp (26 g) coarse sugar

While the biscuits are baking, make the Whipped Honey Ricotta Cream. Over a small bowl, drain the ricotta cheese in a fine-mesh sieve. Allow any liquid to drip into the bowl and discard it. In a large bowl, whip the ricotta cheese with an electric handheld mixer or standing electric mixer until it is thick and fluffy, 4 to 5 minutes. Place the ricotta into a small bowl and set it aside.

Pour the heavy cream and honey into the same bowl where you whipped the ricotta cheese. Whip the cream until stiff peaks form, about 5 minutes. Once the cream has been whipped, fold it into the ricotta cheese and season with the flaky sea salt.

Assemble the shortcakes by slicing the biscuits in half and topping them with the macerated blackberries and a dollop of whipped ricotta. Close the shortcake with the top half of the biscuit. Serve the shortcakes chilled. The shortcakes can be stored in the refrigerator, covered, for 4 to 5 days.

Whipped Honey Ricotta Cream

1 cup (250 g) whole milk ricotta cheese

¼ cup (60 ml) heavy cream

1 tbsp (15 ml) honey

¼ tsp flaky sea salt

Hummingbird Bread with Cream Cheese Frosting

The word "hummingbird" has such a whimsical charm that seamlessly matches the essence of living a simple cottage life. The hummingbird cake, made with juicy pineapple and sweet bananas, originated in beautiful Jamaica. This bread recipe is inspired by that very cake, with a luscious fruity flavor and a wonderfully moist texture! It is a perfect way to add a touch of variety to your usual banana bread baking routine. Don't forget a generous dollop of cream cheese frosting!

Preheat the oven to 350°F (177°C). Grease and flour either one 9 x 5–inch (23 x 13–cm) loaf pan or four 5 x 3–inch (13 x 8–cm) mini loaf pans. Set these aside.

Begin by making the Hummingbird Bread. In a large bowl, whisk together the flour, baking soda, salt, cinnamon, and nutmeg until well combined. Set this aside.

In the bowl of a standing electric mixer fitted with a paddle attachment, cream together the butter, granulated sugar, and brown sugar until the butter has turned pale yellow and the mixture is fluffy, 3 to 4 minutes. Scrape the sides and bottom of the bowl well. Mix in the eggs, fully incorporating each before adding the next, then stir in the vanilla.

Stir in the dry ingredients mixture until there are no longer any dry bits, 2 to 3 minutes. Finally, stir in the mashed banana, crushed pineapple, shredded coconut, and chopped walnuts until the batter is just combined, about 2 minutes.

Spread the batter evenly in the prepared baking pan(s) and bake the bread for 35 to 40 minutes for the mini loaves or 55 to 60 minutes for the single loaf. Let the bread cool in the pan(s) for at least 10 minutes before moving it to a wire cooling rack to finish cooling.

Meanwhile, make the Cream Cheese Frosting. In the bowl of a standing electric mixer fitted with a paddle attachment, cream together the butter, cream cheese, vanilla, and salt until smooth, 2 to 3 minutes. Mix in the powdered sugar until the frosting is smooth and spreadable, another minute.

Once they are fully cooled, spread the cream cheese frosting over the loaf or loaves. Decorate the tops with extra walnuts. Serve the bread at room temperature. If you are saving the bread for later, cover it with plastic wrap and store in your refrigerator until ready to serve.

Makes 1 large loaf or 4 mini loaves

Hummingbird Bread

2½ cups (312 g) all-purpose flour

1 tsp baking soda

½ tsp kosher salt

1 tsp ground cinnamon

¼ tsp ground nutmeg

½ cup (116 g) salted butter, softened

½ cup (100 g) granulated sugar

½ cup (97 g) light brown sugar, packed

2 large eggs

2 tsp (10 ml) vanilla extract

1 cup (198 g) mashed banana, 2 to 3 large bananas

8 oz (226 g) crushed pineapple

1 cup (93 g) sweetened shredded coconut

⅓ cup (35 g) chopped walnuts

Cream Cheese Frosting

½ cup (116 g) salted butter, softened

8 oz (226 g) cream cheese, softened

1 tsp vanilla extract

Pinch of kosher salt

1 cup (118 g) powdered sugar, sifted

Whole walnuts, for decorating

Sweetheart Chocolate Chunk Scones

There is nothing quite as sweet as baking up a batch of yummy scones for your sweetheart or loved ones. These scones are light and fluffy, pairing perfectly with a generous chocolate chunk filling. They are named "sweetheart" scones because they are cut into hearts rather than a round or square shape. These little coffee or tea time treats bake up in under an hour, making them the perfect accompaniment to your morning or afternoon slow living routine.

Preheat the oven to 400°F (204°C). Line a large baking sheet with parchment paper and set it aside.

In a large bowl, whisk together the flour, sugar, baking powder, and salt. With a pastry blender or fork, cut the cubed butter into the dry ingredients until it resembles coarse crumbs about the size of a pea.

With a wooden spoon or silicone spatula, stir in a ½ cup (120 ml) of the heavy cream and the vanilla until the dough begins to come together. At this point, fold in the chocolate chunks with your hands until the dough is uniform and no longer has any dry, crumbly bits, 3 to 4 minutes. Lay the dough out on a lightly floured surface. Fold the dough over itself seven times, creating the scones' layers.

With a rolling pin, roll the dough out to about ½ inch (1.3 cm) thick. With a heart-shaped cookie cutter, cut straight down into the dough without twisting. This will help the scones to rise while baking. If there is leftover dough, bring it back together with your hands and repeat the cutting out process. Place the scones about 2 inches (5 cm) apart on the ungreased baking sheet. Place the baking sheet of scones into the fridge to chill for about 30 minutes.

After the chilling period, brush the tops of the scones with the remaining 2 tablespoons (30 ml) of heavy cream and sprinkle the tops with the coarse sugar. Bake the scones for 12 to 14 minutes, or until they are light golden brown in color and baked through the middle or no longer gooey inside.

Serve the scones hot or at room temperature with a cup of tea or coffee. To store the scones, keep them in an airtight container at room temperature for 4 to 5 days.

Makes about
12 to 14 scones

3 cups (375 g) all-purpose flour, plus more for dusting

¼ cup (50 g) granulated sugar

3 tsp (14 g) baking powder

½ tsp kosher salt

½ cup (116 g) salted butter, cold and cut into ½-inch (1.3-cm) cubes

½ cup (120 ml) + 2 tbsp (30 ml) heavy cream, divided

¼ tsp vanilla extract

½ cup (84 g) semisweet chocolate chunks

1 tbsp (13 g) coarse sugar, for sprinkling

Cherry Almond Scones with Cherry Icing

Wonderfully sweet and filled with notes of almond flavor, these scones are perfect for dunking into hot cups of cream-filled English breakfast tea. These American-style scones are cut into wedges for a lovely presentation. The cherries inside are rehydrated, making them the ideal winter bake when fresh fruit is scarce—this also helps the berries from sinking while baking. Add a delicate drizzle of blush pink icing to the charming tops and you will have a stunning breakfast or afternoon indulgence!

To rehydrate the cherries, in a small saucepan, bring the water to a boil. Place the dried cherries in a medium bowl and pour the boiling water over them, making sure that all of the cherries are covered. Let the cherries sit and soak in the water for about 30 minutes. Drain any excess water.

Now prepare to make the dough for the Cherry Almond Scones. Preheat the oven to 425°F (218°C). Line a large baking sheet with parchment paper and set it aside.

In a large bowl, whisk together the flour, sugar, baking powder, baking soda, and salt. With a pastry blender or fork, cut the cubed butter into the dry ingredients until it resembles coarse crumbs about the size of a pea. Make a well in the center of crumbs and add the ½ cup (120 ml) of heavy cream, the buttermilk, almond extract, and soaked cherries. Stir the mixture with a wooden spoon until it comes together into a shaggy dough, about 2 minutes.

With your hands, knead the dough into a ball, folding it over itself about seven times.

On a lightly floured surface, pat or roll the dough out into a 12-inch (30-cm) circle, about ½ inch (1.3 cm) thick. With a sharp knife, cut the dough into eight wedges, slicing straight down through the dough. Arrange the wedges about 2 inches (5 cm) apart on the baking sheet. Brush the tops of the scones with the remaining 2 tablespoons (30 ml) of heavy cream. Sprinkle the tops with the coarse sugar. Place the scones into the refrigerator for about 30 minutes before baking.

Bake the scones for 15 to 16 minutes, or until they are a light golden brown and are no longer doughy in the middle. Let the scones rest on a wire cooling rack until they are room temperature before icing.

To make the Cherry Icing, whisk together the powdered sugar, cherry juice, milk, and almond extract in a small bowl until the icing is smooth like molasses, about 2 minutes.

Drizzle the icing over the cooled scones. Serve the scones at room temperature or slightly warmed. They can be stored in an airtight container at room temperature for 4 to 5 days.

Makes 8 scones

Cherry Almond Scones

½ cup (120 ml) water

1 cup (160 g) dried cherries

2⅓ cups (292 g) all-purpose flour, plus more for dusting

¾ cup (150 g) granulated sugar

½ tsp baking powder

½ tsp baking soda

½ tsp kosher salt

½ cup (116 g) salted butter, cold and cut into ½-inch (1.3-cm) cubes

½ cup (120 ml) + 2 tbsp (30 ml) heavy cream, divided

¼ cup (60 ml) buttermilk

½ tsp almond extract

2 tbsp (26 g) coarse sugar, for sprinkling

Cherry Icing

1 cup (118 g) powdered sugar

1 tsp maraschino cherry juice

1 tsp whole milk

½ tsp almond extract

Sweet Potato Sage Biscuits

When fall arrives you can find comfort in the warm, rich tones of winter squash and bright orange sweet potatoes, freshly harvested from the soil. The combination of this deliciously sweet vegetable and earthy sage creates an enchanting, autumnal, savory biscuit. Serve this alongside a big bowl of hearty soup for the coziest of meals, perfect for imagining yourself in a little log cabin in a magical, autumnal forest.

Preheat the oven to 425°F (218° C). Set aside a large baking sheet.

In a large bowl, whisk together the flour, sugar, baking powder, baking soda, and salt. Cut in the cold butter with a pastry blender or fork until the mixture resembles coarse crumbs about the size of a pea.

Stir in the mashed sweet potatoes and buttermilk with a wooden spoon or silicone spatula. Sprinkle the fresh sage over the dough and bring it together with your hands until it is no longer dry and crumbly, about 2 minutes. On a lightly floured surface, fold the dough over itself about seven times to create layers in the dough.

Roll or press the dough out flat with your hands until it is about ½ inch (1.3 cm) thick and cut out the biscuits with a 3-inch (8-cm) round biscuit cutter. Be sure to cut straight down through the dough and do not twist the biscuit cutter. Alternately, you can cut the biscuits into shapes like diamonds or squares with a sharp knife, if you prefer something different!

Arrange the cut biscuits on the baking sheet, about 2 inches (5 cm) apart. Place the baking sheet into the refrigerator for about 30 minutes to chill the dough again before baking. Once ready to bake, brush the tops of the biscuits with the melted butter. Arrange sage leaves on top for decoration.

Bake the biscuits for about 20 minutes, or until they are a deep orange color and cooked through the middle. You can check their doneness by gently pulling apart the layers on one of the biscuits to see if they are still doughy or not. Serve the biscuits hot!

To store the biscuits, keep them in an airtight container at room temperature for 4 to 5 days.

Makes about 16 biscuits

4½ cups (563 g) all-purpose flour, plus more for dusting

2 tbsp (30 g) granulated sugar

4 tsp (18 g) baking powder

2 tsp (9 g) baking soda

1 tsp kosher salt

1 cup (232 g) salted butter, cold and cut into ½-inch (1.3-cm) cubes

1 cup (210 g) cold mashed sweet potatoes

½ cup (120 ml) buttermilk

2 tbsp (4 g) fresh chopped sage

2 tbsp (30 ml) melted salted butter

Whole sage leaves, for decorating

Orange Cardamom Yogurt Bread

Lightly spiced and deliciously moist, this orange quick bread is made with Greek yogurt and fresh orange juice to create an incredibly tart and fresh taste. Quick breads made with orange juice were quite popular in the 1920s and 1930s. This bread is perfect to serve for an afternoon snack or breakfast treat decorated with citrus slices, such as clementines or blood oranges. Each slice brings a lovely, rich color to the table that is absolute eye candy. Don't forget to drizzle the top with a simple powdered sugar icing for an extra delicious addition!

Preheat the oven to 350°F (177°C). Grease an 8½ x 4½ x 2⅝–inch (22 x 11 x 8–cm) loaf pan and set this aside.

Begin by making the Orange Cardamom Yogurt Bread. In a large bowl, whisk together the flour, baking powder, cinnamon, cardamom, salt, and brown sugar. Add the eggs, melted butter, yogurt, orange juice, orange zest, and vanilla and stir with a wooden spoon or spatula until the batter comes together and there are no longer any visible lumps, 2 to 4 minutes. Be careful to not overmix the batter.

Spread the batter evenly into the prepared pan. Bake the orange loaf for 40 to 45 minutes, or until a toothpick inserted in the center comes out clean. Immediately invert the loaf onto a wire cooling rack and let the bread cool to room temperature.

In a small bowl, make the Orange Powdered Sugar Icing. Whisk together the powdered sugar, orange juice, and orange zest until the icing is the consistency of maple syrup, about 2 minutes.

Drizzle the icing over the cooled bread and decorate the top with a sprinkle of cardamom or cinnamon and clementine and orange slices. If you are saving the bread for later, cover the bread with plastic wrap and store in your refrigerator until ready to serve. It can be stored for about 4 to 5 days.

Makes 1 loaf

Orange Cardamom Yogurt Bread

2 cups (250 g) all-purpose flour

2½ tsp (11 g) baking powder

1 tsp ground cinnamon, plus more for decorating

1 tsp ground cardamom, plus more for decorating

½ tsp kosher salt

½ cup (97 g) light brown sugar, packed

2 large eggs

½ cup (120 ml) melted salted butter, cooled slightly

½ cup (120 ml) plain Greek yogurt

¾ cup (180 ml) fresh orange juice, about 2 large oranges

2 tbsp (15 g) orange zest

2 tsp (10 ml) vanilla extract

Orange Powdered Sugar Icing

1 cup (118 g) powdered sugar, sifted

1 tbsp (15 ml) fresh orange juice

1 tsp orange zest

Clementine and blood orange slices, for decorating

Bacon, Cheddar, and Herb King Cornmeal Muffins

You will love these jumbo-sized muffins that hold in all of the flavor! These cornmeal muffins are made the old-fashioned way, with bacon fat for a pleasurable hint of smoky saltiness. This brings a savory twist to one of the oldest foods from North America, using fresh herbs from the garden and sharp yellow cheddar cheese. Somewhere in between a classic cornbread and a cake, these muffins have just the right amount of sweet and salty to make them your favorite side dish to accompany a bowl of soup or salad.

In a large skillet, fry the bacon until crispy, 7 to 10 minutes. Place the bacon on a paper towel–lined plate to cool and drain and reserve 4 tablespoons (60 ml) of the bacon fat. Once the bacon has cooled down enough to handle, chop it into small bits about the size of a pea. Set this aside while you make the muffins.

Preheat the oven to 400°F (204°C) and grease a king-sized or jumbo muffin tin. Set this aside.

In a large bowl whisk together the flour, cornmeal, granulated sugar, brown sugar, baking powder, salt, and pepper. Make a well in the center of the dry ingredients and add the eggs, buttermilk, cheese, parsley, dill, and chives. Stir everything together until the mixture is no longer dry, about 2 minutes. Then, fold in the melted butter and the reserved bacon fat until the batter is no longer separated, another 2 to 3 minutes. Stir in the chopped bacon bits.

Divide the batter evenly between the muffin cups, filling them about three-quarters of the way full. Bake the muffins for 25 to 30 minutes, or until a toothpick inserted in the center comes out clean. Let the muffins rest in the tin for about 10 minutes before moving to a wire cooling rack to finish cooling.

Serve the muffins with flaky sea salt and whipped butter. To store the muffins, keep them in an airtight container at room temperature for 4 to 5 days.

*Makes about
6 king-sized muffins*

8 slices (112 g) applewood smoked bacon

2½ cups (312 g) all-purpose flour

2 cups (260 g) yellow cornmeal

½ cup (100 g) granulated sugar

½ cup (98 g) light brown sugar, packed

3 tsp (14 g) baking powder

1 tsp kosher salt

1 tsp freshly cracked black pepper

2 large eggs

2 cups (480 ml) buttermilk

2 cups (226 g) sharp cheddar cheese, shredded

2 tbsp (4 g) fresh parsley, chopped

2 tbsp (4 g) fresh dill, chopped

4 tsp (2 g) fresh chives, chopped

4 tbsp (60 ml) melted salted butter

Flaky sea salt, for serving

Whipped butter, for serving

Country Garden Pies and Tarts

After a long day of picking fruit from the local orchard, it's wonderful to spend time in the kitchen baking with your haul of fresh blueberries, strawberries, raspberries, peaches, or apples. Baking pies is one way that I have always felt I could easily romanticize my time spent in the kitchen, rolling out pie crust with my great grandma's rolling pin and licking sweet berry juices from my fingertips.

The art of pie baking has been around since ancient times, and some of the earliest pies were filled with honey and foraged fruits. As our recipes evolved, pies were made with sturdy crusts and filled with savory ingredients like game or fish, and eventually it became a cottage industry with both sweet and savory pies made for formal and informal occasions. Today, pie making is a beloved pastime. The aroma of a freshly baked pie or tart is sure to evoke feelings of comfort and nostalgia, and this is a testament to the charming appeal of this timeless treat.

In this chapter, you will find the cutest pie and tart creations to feed your sentimental yearning, like the Mixed Berry Wildflower Pop Tarts (page 29); Peach, Rhubarb, and Basil Pie (page 35); and Tea Party Strawberry Tartlets (page 40). For something on the more decadent side, you might prefer the Dark Chocolate Tarte Bourdaloue (page 31) or Old-Fashioned Oatmeal Pecan Pie (page 37). Don't forget to try a savory pie like the Beef, Mushroom, and Stout Pie (page 43) to feed your hobbit heart!

Mixed Berry Wildflower Pop Tarts

Edible flowers make everything beautiful! You can easily grow your own edible flower garden to use for baking, and they look so pretty drying in the house. With a little bit of imagination, you can create magical baked goods with just a few sprinkles of lavender or calendula and transform what was once ordinary into something truly special. These mixed berry pop tarts taste like your favorite childhood breakfast treat, with a touch of brightly colored flower petals for added whimsy!

First, make the Pie Crust. In a medium bowl, whisk together the flour, sugar, and salt. With a pastry blender or fork, cut in the cubed butter until it resembles coarse crumbs about the size of a pea, about 4 minutes. Spoon the cold water over the crumbs, stirring in only about 1 tablespoon (15 ml) at a time, until the dough begins to come together. It may be a bit crumbly, so it will have to be kneaded with your hands. Try to touch it as little as possible to prevent the butter from melting. When most of the dryness is gone and the dough holds together on its own, it is ready.

Shape the dough into two discs and wrap them in plastic wrap. Refrigerate the dough for at least 1 hour before shaping.

Bring the dough out of the refrigerator and let it sit on the counter for about 10 minutes to soften slightly. On a lightly floured surface, roll out one of the dough discs into a 10 x 20–inch (25 x 50–cm) rectangle. With a sharp knife, slice the rectangle into two 5 x 20–inch (13 x 50–cm) halves. Then, slice into about nine 5 x 3–inch (13 x 8–cm) rectangles. Trim off any rough edges so that the rectangles are perfectly square. Repeat with the other half of the dough until you have 18 rectangles total. Lay the pieces of dough onto a large baking sheet lined with parchment paper and pop them into the refrigerator for 35 to 40 minutes to chill the butter.

Meanwhile, make the Mixed Berry Jam Filling. In a large saucepan, bring the strawberries, blueberries, raspberries, sugar, lemon juice, and lemon zest to a boil and cook for 8 to 10 minutes. Stir and boil the jam, lowering the heat to about medium, until it begins to thicken and runs off of a tilted spoon in a single sheet rather than a quick drizzly stream. You can also test the doneness of the jam if it has reached a temperature of 220°F (105°C). Remove the pan from the heat and let the jam cool until it is comfortable to the touch.

(continued)

Makes about 9 tarts

Pie Crust

2½ cups (312 g) all-purpose flour

2 tbsp (30 g) granulated sugar

1 tsp kosher salt

1 cup (232 g) salted butter, cold and cut into ½-inch (1.3-cm) cubes

6 tbsp (90 ml) ice water

Mixed Berry Jam Filling

1 cup (166 g) fresh strawberries, chopped

½ cup (78 g) fresh blueberries

½ cup (62 g) fresh raspberries

1½ cups (300 g) granulated sugar

1 tbsp (15 ml) fresh lemon juice

2 tsp (5 g) fresh lemon zest

Preheat the oven to 375°F (191°C). Remove the tart dough from the fridge and bring the baking sheet to the countertop. Spoon about 2 tablespoons (30 ml) of jam onto the middle of one of the pieces of tart dough. With a second piece of tart dough, cover the jam and crimp the edges together with the tines of a fork. Repeat with the remaining jam and tarts. With the tines of the fork, poke about four sets of holes into the tops of the pop tarts to let air escape.

In a small bowl, whisk together the egg and water to make the egg wash. Brush the egg wash all over the tops of the pop tarts. Bake the pop tarts for 25 to 30 minutes, or until they are a deep golden brown and the filling inside is bubbly and hot. Let the pop tarts cool completely before icing.

To make the White Chocolate Coating, bring a small saucepan of water to a simmer on the stovetop. Place a small heat-safe bowl over the simmering water and add in the white chocolate chips and coconut oil. Stir until all of the chocolate is melted and the oil has blended well with the chocolate, 3 to 4 minutes. Remove the bowl from over the saucepan and onto the counter-top. If using, stir in the food coloring until your desired color is reached.

Place the baked pop tarts on a wire cooling rack situated over a baking sheet lined with parchment paper to catch any choco-late drippings. Pour the White Chocolate Coating evenly over each of the tops of the pop tarts. While the chocolate is still warm, sprinkle it with the dried lavender and dried calendula. Let the chocolate harden before serving.

To store, keep the pop tarts at room temperature in an airtight container for 4 to 5 days.

1 large egg + 1 tbsp (15 ml) water, for egg wash

White Chocolate Coating

½ cup (84 g) white chocolate chips

1 tbsp (15 ml) coconut oil

Violet food coloring, optional

1 tbsp (6 g) dried, food-grade lavender

1 tbsp (6 g) dried, food-grade calendula petals

Dark Chocolate Tarte Bourdaloue

This tart is a true indulgence, perfect for an evening spent by the fireside. The juicy pears are poached in Cabernet Sauvignon or rustic apple cider and spiced with cinnamon and star anise, creating a warming flavor that feels like a hug. The pears are then nestled into a delicious dark chocolate and almond frangipane filling, which is baked in a chocolate shortcrust pastry that crumbles with each bite. It's exactly what you need to satisfy all of your chocolate cravings! Make this for a romantic candlelit evening underneath the glow of the moon and stars.

Begin by preparing the Chocolate Shortcrust. In a large bowl, combine the flour, cocoa powder, sugar, and salt with a whisk. With a pastry blender or fork, cut in the butter until it forms small crumbles. Continue to work in the butter with your fingers, smashing it flat, until the mixture resembles breadcrumbs. Once the butter has been cut in, add the egg and cold water and stir together the crust with a wooden spoon or silicone spatula. As the dough comes together, it may be easier to work it with your hands, kneading until it is smooth, about 5 minutes. This crust is rather dry at first but it will eventually come together.

Shape the dough into a disc and wrap it tightly with plastic wrap. Refrigerate the dough for at least 1 hour. Once chilled, bring the dough out onto the counter and let it rest for about 10 minutes. Unwrap the dough and roll it out into a 12-inch (30-cm) circle. Set aside an ungreased 11-inch (28-cm) tart pan.

Carefully wrap the shortcrust over the rolling pin, then lift the rolling pin by the handles up and over the tart pan. Unroll the shortcrust over the top of the tart pan and press it into the bottom of the pan and up the sides, shaping it into the grooves. There should be about a 1-inch (2.5-cm) overhang. Simply roll the rolling pin over the top of the tart pan to cut this off and create a perfect edge to the crust. Prick the bottom of the crust all over with a fork.

Cover the crust with plastic wrap and refrigerate for another 30 minutes to 1 hour. Alternately, it can be kept in the fridge for about 2 days or frozen to use later.

Preheat the oven to 350°F (177°C). Line the crust with aluminum foil and fill the foil with pie weights or dried beans all the way up the sides of the pan. Bake the crust for 15 minutes. Remove the pie weights and foil.

Whisk together the egg and water for the egg wash in a small dish and brush the entire crust with the egg wash. Bake the crust for another 10 minutes. Set the crust aside to cool a bit while you make the filling.

(continued)

Makes 1 (11-inch [28-cm]) tart

Chocolate Shortcrust

1¾ cups (218 g) all-purpose flour

¼ cup (25 g) Dutch cocoa powder

2 tbsp (30 g) granulated sugar

¼ tsp kosher salt

½ cup (116 g) salted butter, cold and cut into ½-inch (1.3-cm) cubes

1 large egg

2 tbsp (30 ml) ice cold water

1 large egg + 1 tbsp (15 ml) water, for egg wash

While the crust bakes, make the Red Wine–Poached Pears. In a large saucepan, bring the water, red wine, and sugar to a boil. Whisk the liquid until the sugar dissolves. Lower the heat to a simmer and stir in the almond extract, cinnamon sticks, star anise, and pears. Stir the mixture gently and occasionally for about 15 minutes. Turn off the heat and drain the pears on a plate to cool. Reserve about ¼ cup (60 ml) of the red wine syrup.

As the pears cool to room temperature, make the Dark Chocolate Frangipane Filling. In a large bowl, cream the butter and sugar until light and fluffy, 4 to 5 minutes. Whisk in the beaten eggs and almond extract until well blended, 1 to 2 minutes. Fold in the almond flour, all-purpose flour, and salt. Once the filling becomes creamy and smooth, about 2 minutes, fold in the melted chocolate until the filling is a light brown and no longer has streaks, about 1 minute.

Spread the Dark Chocolate Frangipane Filling in the par-baked shortcrust, smoothing it evenly. Carefully cut the pears in half lengthwise, keeping the stems attached. Place the poached pears on top of the frangipane filling, arranging them in a circle with the slimmer end facing the center of the tart. With a sharp paring knife, slice the pears horizontally into thin or thick slices. Gently press the sliced almonds into the filling around the pears.

Bake the tart for 55 to 60 minutes, or until the filling is set, and there is no longer any liquid sitting around the pears. Let the tart rest for about 10 minutes before removing the outside of the tart pan. Brush the finished tart with the reserved red wine syrup. Slice the tart into six pieces and serve with whipped cream.

To store, keep the tart covered in the refrigerator for 4 to 5 days.

Red Wine–Poached Pears

1¼ cups (300 ml) water

1¼ cups (300 ml) dry red wine, such as Cabernet Sauvignon, or apple cider

1 cup (200 g) granulated sugar

1 tsp almond extract

2 cinnamon sticks (12 g)

1 star anise (2 g)

3 large firm pears (902 g), peeled

Dark Chocolate Frangipane Filling

1 cup (232 g) salted butter, softened

1 cup (200 g) granulated sugar

4 large eggs, lightly beaten

2 tsp (10 ml) almond extract

1½ cups (162 g) almond flour

½ cup (63 g) all-purpose flour

1 tsp kosher salt

4 oz (113 g) dark chocolate, melted and slightly cooled

½ cup (44 g) sliced almonds

Whipped cream, for serving

Peach, Rhubarb, and Basil Pie

Oh, how we adore the sweet and juicy peaches of summertime! Paired with tart rhubarb and fragrant, fresh basil, they create a truly unique and earthy flavor that will make your tastebuds dance with joy. Just imagine serving a slice of this gorgeous pie under the dappled shade of a fruit tree, with the gentle hum of bees and a refreshing glass of homemade lemonade. The pretty lattice crust, with its delicate pattern of interwoven pastry, adds an extra touch of whimsy and charm to this already delightful dessert. Soak in the warm sunshine and revel in the simple pleasures of summer in the countryside.

First, make the Pie Crust. In a medium bowl, whisk together the flour, sugar, and salt. With a pastry blender or fork, cut in the cubed butter until it resembles coarse crumbs about the size of a pea. This takes about 4 minutes. Spoon the cold water over the crumbs, stirring in only about 1 tablespoon (15 ml) at a time, until the dough begins to come together. It may be a bit crumbly, so it will have to be kneaded with your hands. Try to touch it as little as possible to prevent the butter from melting. When most of the dryness is gone and the dough holds together on its own, it is ready. Shape the dough into two discs and wrap them in plastic wraps. Refrigerate the dough for at least 1 hour before shaping.

Preheat the oven to 350°F (177°C) and set aside a 10½ x 2½–inch (27 x 6–cm) pie dish.

Bring one half of the dough out of the refrigerator and let it sit on the counter for about 10 minutes to soften slightly. Roll out the dough on a lightly floured work surface to about 12 inches (30 cm) in diameter. Wrap the dough around your rolling pin and lift the pin up by the ends. Place the pin over your pie dish. Unroll the dough over the pie dish and press it into the bottom and sides, being careful not to stretch the dough but rather lifting and moving it down into the dish. Trim along the edges of the dough, leaving a 1-inch (2.5-cm) overhang. Fold the edge under about ½ inch (1.3 cm) and press it together to create a smooth, rounded edge. With your fingers, flute the edges around the pie for a decorative look. Poke holes all over the bottom of the crust with a fork. Return the shaped dough to the refrigerator while you make the Peach Rhubarb Basil Filling.

(continued)

Makes 1 (10-inch [25-cm]) pie

Pie Crust

2½ cups (312 g) all-purpose flour, plus more for dusting

2 tbsp (30 g) granulated sugar

1 tsp kosher salt

1 cup (232 g) salted butter, cold and cut into ½-inch (1.3-cm) cubes

6 tbsp (90 ml) ice water

In a small saucepan, bring enough water to cover the peaches to a boil. Set aside a medium-sized bowl of ice water. Slice an "X" on the bottom of each peach and boil them in the water, 1 to 2 minutes. Remove the peaches from the boiling water with a slotted spoon and immediately dunk them into a bath of ice water. When the peaches are cool enough to handle, slip off the skins. Discard the skins and slice the peaches in half, revealing the pit. Remove the pit, then slice the peaches into ½-inch (1.3-cm) slices.

In a large bowl, toss together the sliced peaches, rhubarb chunks, basil leaves, sugar, cornstarch, cinnamon, nutmeg, salt, and egg. Mix everything until the fruit is well coated, about 2 minutes.

Once the filling has been mixed, prepare the top pie crust. Dust the countertop lightly with flour. Take out the second disc of pie crust and roll it out to a 12-inch (30-cm) circle. Cut the crust into strips for a lattice top, about ½ inch (1.3 cm) in width. Trim off any uneven edges.

Meanwhile, mix together the egg and water for the egg wash. Bring out the lined pie dish and brush the entire crust with the egg wash. Fill the pie crust with the peach filling and dot the top of the filling with the cubed butter.

Arrange the lattice on the top of the pie crust. If you have extra pie crust, you may want to cut out designs like leaves or flowers for decoration. Finally, brush the lattice with the egg wash and dust the top of the pie with the coarse sugar.

Place the pie dish on a large baking sheet and bake the pie for 50 to 60 minutes, or until the crust is a deep golden brown and the filling is bubbly and thickened. If necessary, cover the top of the pie with foil for the final 15 minutes of baking to prevent it from over-browning. Let the pie rest for at least 30 minutes before slicing.

To store, keep the pie covered at room temperature or in the refrigerator for 4 to 5 days.

Peach Rhubarb Basil Filling

½ lb (226 g) fresh peaches

2 cups (260 g) fresh rhubarb, chopped into 1-inch (2.5-cm) chunks

½ cup (20 g) fresh basil leaves, chopped

1 cup (200 g) granulated sugar

2 tbsp (16 g) cornstarch

1 tsp ground cinnamon

¼ tsp ground nutmeg

Pinch of kosher salt

1 large egg

1 large egg + 1 tbsp (15 ml) water, for egg wash

¼ cup (29 g) salted butter, cold and cut into ½-inch (1-cm) cubes

1 tbsp (13 g) coarse sugar, for dusting

Old-Fashioned Oatmeal Pecan Pie

Perfectly rustic and wonderfully spiced, this old-fashioned pecan pie becomes an instantly unique dessert with the addition of rolled oats. The concept of the oatmeal pie has been around, presumably, since the American Civil War era as a way to create a similar flavor and texture of a pecan pie when pecans were scarcely available. If you are looking for something that feels like a warm hug on a chilly day in your favorite little cozy village, you will love this recipe for its flaky, buttery crust and chewy oatmeal texture.

First, make the Pie Crust. In a medium bowl, whisk together the flour, sugar, and salt. With a pastry blender or fork, cut in the cubed butter until it resembles coarse crumbs, about the size of a pea. This takes about 4 minutes. Spoon the cold water over the crumbs, stirring in only about 1 tablespoon (15 ml) at a time, until the dough begins to come together. It may be a bit crumbly, so it will have to be kneaded with your hands. Try to touch it as little as possible to prevent the butter from melting. When most of the dryness is gone and the dough holds together on its own, it is ready. Shape the dough into a disc and wrap it in plastic wrap. Refrigerate the dough for at least 1 hour before shaping.

Preheat the oven to 350°F (177°C) and set aside a 10½ x 2½–inch (27 x 6–cm) pie dish.

Bring the dough out of the refrigerator and let it sit on the counter for about 10 minutes to soften slightly. Roll out the dough on a lightly floured work surface to about 12 inches (30 cm) in diameter. Wrap the dough around your rolling pin and lift the pin up by the ends. Place the pin over your pie dish. Unroll the dough over the pie dish and press it into the bottom and sides, being careful not to stretch the dough but rather lifting and moving it down into the dish. Trim along the edges of the dough, leaving a 1-inch (2.5-cm) overhang. Fold the edge under about ½ inch (1.3 cm) and press it together to create a smooth, rounded edge. With the tines of a fork, press a design into the edges of the crust. Poke holes all over the bottom of the crust with the fork.

At this point, you may par-bake the crust if it is still chilled. If the dough is too warm, place it in the refrigerator for about 20 minutes. Once chilled again, line the inside of the pie crust with parchment paper and fill the parchment with pie weights or dried beans. Fill the pie all the way to the top. Bake the pie for about 15 minutes, or until it is lightly yellowed. Remove the pie weights and bake for another 10 minutes. Remove the pie from the oven and let it cool slightly.

(continued)

Makes 1 (10-inch [25-cm]) pie

Pie Crust

1¼ cups (156 g) all-purpose flour

1 tbsp (15 g) granulated sugar

½ tsp kosher salt

½ cup (116 g) salted butter, cold and cut into ½-inch (1.3-cm) cubes

3 to 4 tbsp (45 to 60 ml) ice water

While the crust cools, make the Oatmeal Pecan Filling. In a large bowl, whisk the eggs, brown sugar, and granulated sugar until pale yellow and syrupy, about 4 minutes. Set this aside. In a small saucepan, brown the butter by melting it over medium-low heat and simmering it until it begins to turn brown in color with a nutty aroma, about 10 minutes. Remove the butter from the heat and let it cool slightly.

Stir the browned butter, flour, salt, cinnamon, nutmeg, heavy cream, vanilla, 1 cup (100 g) of the pecans, and the oats into the egg mixture. In a small bowl, whisk together the egg and water for the egg wash. Brush this all over the pie crust, including in all of the little grooves around the edge of the pie. Pour the filling into the pie, spreading it evenly. With the remaining ½ cup (50 g) of pecans, place them around the edge of the pie in a large ring, floating on the surface of the filling.

Bake the pie for 40 to 50 minutes, or until the top has formed a brown crust, the edges are set, and the center jiggles slightly like Jell-O™. Let the pie rest on the counter for 3 to 4 hours before slicing. To serve, decorate the pie with piped whipped cream and extra pecans. To store, cover the pie and keep at room temperature for 4 to 5 days.

Oatmeal Pecan Filling

3 large eggs

1½ cups (291 g) dark brown sugar, packed

½ cup (100 g) granulated sugar

¾ cup (174 g) salted butter

2 tbsp (12 g) all-purpose flour

½ tsp kosher salt

1 tsp ground cinnamon

¼ tsp ground nutmeg

2 tbsp (30 ml) heavy cream

2 tsp (10 ml) vanilla extract

1½ cups (150 g) pecan halves, divided

1 cup (84 g) rolled oats

1 egg + 1 tbsp (15 ml) water, for egg wash

Whipped cream, for serving

Extra pecans, for decorating

Tea Party Strawberry Tartlets

There is something so charming about a perfectly baked tartlet. Each bite is a heavenly mix of buttery crust, creamy filling, and juicy strawberries that burst with flavor. The delicate, flaky pastry is perfectly complemented by the sweet tart flavors of the strawberries and the dreamy strawberry cream. When it is time to serve the tartlets, decorate the tops with brightly colored fresh fruit and tiny edible flowers for a final presentation that is sure to steal the hearts of all your tea party guests. Share them with your loved ones, or enjoy them all to yourself as you bask in the warm glow of a lazy summer afternoon.

Begin by making the Sweet Pastry Tart Shells. In a food processor or blender, combine the all-purpose flour, almond flour, powdered sugar, and salt and pulse a few times to fully mix together the ingredients. Add the butter and continue to pulse, on high speed, until the mixture resembles sand. The crumbles should be small and all of the butter should be coated well with the dry ingredients, about 4 minutes.

Slowly add in the beaten egg, pulsing as you add it. The dough should be soft and a bit sticky, resembling something like sugar cookie dough. Remove the dough from the food processor and shape it into a small rectangle as best as you can with your hands. Wrap the dough loosely in plastic wrap and roll it out on your countertop until it is a large rectangle, about 6 x 10 inches (15 x 25 cm). Place the wrapped dough in the refrigerator and chill the dough for at least 2 hours or overnight. The longer the dough chills, the better it will taste and the easier it will be to work with.

On the day that you plan to bake the tart shells, grease nine 3-inch (8-cm) perforated tart rings with butter. Line two baking sheets with silicone mesh baking mats or parchment paper. Set these aside.

After the chilling period, when the dough is cold and firm, unwrap it and place it on a generously floured work surface. Flour the dough on all sides, as it will warm up quickly and easily stick to the countertop. Divide the dough into two pieces. Wrap and refrigerate one piece while you work with the other half.

Roll out the dough so that it has about a ½-inch (1.3-cm) thickness across the dough. It should be thin enough that you can see through the dough slightly. With the greased tart rings, cut out 18 circles for the bottoms of the tarts. You may knead the dough back together as needed to roll and cut out more circles. Arrange the tart rings on the prepared baking sheets. Carefully drop the cut-out circles of tart dough into the bottoms of the rings and set these aside.

Makes about 9 tarts

Sweet Pastry Tart Shells

1⅓ cups (167 g) all-purpose flour

¼ cup (27 g) almond flour

¾ cup (89 g) powdered sugar

Pinch of kosher salt

5 tbsp (73 g) salted butter, cold and cut into ½-inch (1.3-cm) cubes

1 large egg, lightly beaten

Roll out the other half of the tart dough to the same thickness. Cut out strips of pastry about 1½ inches (4 cm) wide. With your hands, gently press these around the inside of the tart rings, pressing them together with the bottoms of the tarts so that they blend together and create a seal. Try not to press them too much through the perforated rings, the dough should be able to stand on its own. With a sharp paring knife, slice around the edges of the tart rings to create a perfect edge to the tarts. To finish shaping the tarts, poke holes all along the bottom of the crust to prevent the tarts from puffing while they bake.

Place the tarts on their baking sheets and in the freezer for 30 minutes. While the crusts are in the freezer, preheat the oven to 350°F (177°C).

After the chilling period, bake the tarts in the preheated oven for 20 to 25 minutes, or until they are golden brown and have shrunken back from the sides of the tart rings. Allow the tarts to cool completely before removing them from the rings. This should be easy, as the rings should simply slide right off from the crusts. Allow the tarts to cool completely before filling.

(continued)

To make the Strawberry Pastry Cream, begin by infusing the milk. Add the milk to a medium saucepan. Then, slicing a vanilla bean in half, scrape out the seeds from one side of the pod with the back of a knife or spoon. Save the other half for another use. Place the scraped seeds into the pan of milk. Place the saucepan over medium-low heat and warm the milk slightly, just until it begins to gently simmer around the edges of the pan. Remove the pan from the heat and cover the pan with a lid, letting the vanilla infuse into the milk for about 10 minutes.

Meanwhile, in a medium bowl, whisk together the egg yolks and sugar until the yolks turn a pale yellow and the mixture becomes thick and syrupy, about 4 minutes. Whisk in the cornstarch until it is no longer visible, another minute.

Once the milk has infused, remove the lid and return the pot to medium-low heat. Once the milk is hot again, pour about 2 tablespoons (30 ml) of the milk into the egg mixture. Immediately whisk the eggs, tempering them. Then, pour the warmed egg mixture back into the pot of hot milk. Cook the custard over medium-low heat, whisking constantly, until the custard begins to thicken. It will thicken considerably, to about the consistency of commercial mayonnaise, 4 to 5 minutes. Continue to whisk until the custard reaches its peak thickness, then it will begin to thin out slightly and look satiny, another 1 to 2 minutes.

Remove the pan from the heat and stir in the butter and strawberry jam. Transfer the custard to a shallow pan, such as a cake pan or pie pan, and cover it with plastic wrap that touches the surface of the custard. Refrigerate the custard until it is completely chilled, about 3 hours.

Before assembling the tarts, make the Macerated Strawberries. Slice the strawberries or cut them into halves, depending on your preference for decorating, and place them in a medium bowl with the sugar. Coat the sliced berries with the sugar and let them rest at room temperature for about 30 minutes.

To assemble the tarts, place the chilled pastry cream into a large piping bag. Cut off the tip and pipe the cream into the baked tart shells all the way to the edge. For a clean edge, use a bench scraper to remove any lumps, being careful not to break the edge of the shells. Decorate the tarts with the slices of Macerated Strawberries and fresh chamomile flowers.

To store the tarts, cover and keep in the refrigerator for 3 to 4 days.

Strawberry Pastry Cream

1 cup (240 ml) whole milk

Half of 1 vanilla bean

3 egg yolks

⅓ cup (66 g) granulated sugar

2 tbsp (16 g) cornstarch

1 tbsp (14 g) salted butter

¼ cup (60 ml) strawberry jam

Macerated Strawberries

1 cup (130 g) fresh, whole strawberries

½ cup (100 g) granulated sugar

Fresh chamomile flowers, for decorating

Beef, Mushroom, and Stout Pie

A little meat pie reminiscent of medieval tavern food, this savory pie brings together all of your favorite hamburger flavors with a deliciously buttery hot water pastry crust. The secret to this pie's enchanting flavor lies in the unique combination of ingredients—tender, succulent beef; earthy mushrooms; and a rich, malty stout. Hot water pastry defies everything you have ever learned about making pie crust, as it is made with boiling hot water and melted butter, rather than everything needing to be chilled. The resulting pastry, though just as flaky, is able to stand on its own while holding all of the inner contents in place. This makes it a really fun recipe for meat pies, especially those with ingredients that are arranged in colorful layers.

Preheat the oven to 400°F (204°C). Grease a 7-inch (18-cm) springform pan heavily with butter and place it on a baking sheet lined with parchment paper. Set this aside.

Begin by making the Hot Water Pastry. In a large bowl, whisk together the all-purpose flour, bread flour, and salt. Set this aside.

In a medium saucepan, bring the butter and water to a boil. Lower the heat to a simmer and continue to cook for about 2 minutes, melting the butter and keeping it very hot. Remove the pan from the heat and immediately pour the hot water and butter into the flour mixture. With a wooden spoon or dough whisk, mix it together until it forms a soft, lumpy dough.

Once the dough is cool enough to handle but still hot, begin to knead it together with your hands until it is smooth. Place the dough onto a lightly floured surface and fold it over itself about three times. Shape the dough into two flat discs and wrap them in plastic wrap. Place them on the counter and let them rest until they are at room temperature. You will want this dough to remain warm to the touch, so keep an eye on it to make sure that it does not get too cold.

While the dough rests, make the filling. In a large skillet over medium-high heat, melt the butter. Add the mushrooms and cook until they turn brown and begin to release their own juices, 5 to 7 minutes. Add the ground beef, onion, and garlic and cook until the beef has been browned all over and the onion is soft and translucent, 5 minutes. Stir in the celery and carrots, cooking until they are slightly softened, about 4 minutes.

Makes 1 (7-inch [18-cm]) pie

Hot Water Pastry

3½ cups (438 g) all-purpose flour

1 cup (138 g) bread flour

1 tsp kosher salt

1 cup (232 g) salted butter, sliced

1 cup (240 ml) water

Beef, Mushroom, and Stout Filling

4 tbsp (58 g) salted butter

2 cups (200 g) brown mushrooms, sliced

1 lb (454 g) ground beef

1 medium yellow onion (234 g), diced

3 cloves (12 g) garlic, minced

3 ribs celery (100 g), diced

2 medium carrots (158 g), peeled and diced

(continued)

Season all of the vegetables and meat with the oregano, thyme, paprika, garlic powder, salt, and pepper. Add the tomato paste, Worcestershire sauce, brown sugar and stir everything to coat. Pour in the stout beer, bringing the mixture to a boil. Lower the heat to a simmer and cook the filling until most of the liquid has been absorbed and it has become a thick sauce, 6 to 8 minutes. Remove the skillet from the heat and let the filling rest, adjusting any seasonings to your liking.

While the filling rests, put the pie together. In a small bowl, whisk together the egg and water to create the egg wash. Set this aside. Divide one of the halves of dough into two equal-sized pieces. Wrap one of those pieces back in plastic wrap.

With the other piece of dough, roll it between two sheets of parchment paper until it is about ½ inch (1.3 cm) thick. With the 7-inch (18-cm) springform pan as a guide, cut out a circular shape for the bottom of the crust to fit inside the pan. Transfer the cut piece of dough to the springform pan and press it into the bottom.

With the second piece of dough that you just wrapped, roll it out to about ½ inch (1.3 cm) thick between two pieces of parchment paper. Cut the dough into 4-inch (10-cm)-wide strips and press these strips around and up the sides of the springform pan. It may be pressed together where needed. The dough must peek out over the top of the pan. Brush the inside of the crust all over with the egg wash. Add the filling to the inside of the crust, spreading it evenly.

With the final piece of wrapped dough, roll it out in a similar fashion between two pieces of parchment, about ½ inch (1.3 cm) thick. Cut the piece of dough into a circle that is large enough to cover the top of the pie and seal together the edges. Lay this over the filling, crimping together the edges of the pie with your finger to enclose it.

With any leftover dough that you may have reserved, roll it out and cut out designs. You may be as creative as you like. Leaves are lovely, as is a braid or a little bird. Don't forget to leave a small hole in the center of the pie to let heat escape!

Brush the top crust of the pie with the egg wash, then layer on the designs. Brush these with more egg wash. Place the baking sheet holding the pie into the preheated oven. Bake the pie for 30 to 35 minutes, or until the crust is golden brown. Gently remove the sides of the springform pan, and then brush the crust all over with any remaining egg wash. Bake for another 10 to 15 minutes.

Remove the pie from the oven and let it rest until it is almost completely cool, 50 to 60 minutes. Slice the pie and serve lukewarm. To store the pie, keep covered with foil in the refrigerator for 4 to 5 days.

2 tsp (2 g) dried oregano

1 tsp dried thyme

1 tsp paprika

½ tsp garlic powder

2 tsp kosher salt

½ tsp freshly cracked black pepper

6 oz (170 g) tomato paste

2 tbsp (30 ml) Worcestershire sauce

1 tbsp (12 g) light brown sugar

12 oz (355 ml) stout beer or beef broth

1 large egg + 1 tbsp (15 ml) water, for egg wash

Butternut Squash, Thyme, and Goat Cheese Hand Pies

These little savory pies fit right in your hand, ideal for an adventurer's or forager's picnic! The perfectly paired butternut squash and goat cheese are seasoned with fresh thyme and flaky sea salt for an autumnal mix. You might imagine these served in a rustic tavern or baked by your granny who lives in the woods. Take these packed inside your basket, as they can be eaten hot or cold. The smells of roasted butternut squash and thyme will bring your senses straight to autumn. Be sure to enjoy these pies with a mug of fresh cider!

Preheat the oven to 425°F (218°C). Line two large baking sheets with parchment paper and set them aside.

Cut off the very top of the head of garlic to expose the cloves inside. Place the garlic head on a small piece of foil and drizzle the olive oil all over, making sure most of it gets inside of the skin and into the cloves. Enclose the garlic head in the foil and place it in a small oven-safe baking dish. Roast the garlic in the oven for 25 to 30 minutes, or until the cloves are very soft. Let the garlic rest until cool enough to handle.

Once the garlic has cooled, squeeze out the cloves into a large bowl. With a potato masher or fork, mash the garlic cloves until they are smooth like a paste. To the mashed garlic, add the butternut squash puree, goat cheese, thyme leaves, sea salt, and pepper.

With a 3-inch (8-cm) biscuit cutter, cut out 24 circles of the puff pastry. Scoop 1 to 2 tablespoons (15 to 30 ml) of the butternut squash filling onto one of the pastry circles, leaving a ½-inch (1.3-cm) border. Brush the edges of the pastry with a bit of water. Enclose the squash filling with another piece of pastry, sealing the edges with the tines of a fork. Poke a few holes into the top of the pastry with the fork as well, to let air escape while baking. Repeat with the remaining pastry and squash filling until all of the pastry has been used.

Arrange the hand pies on the prepared baking sheets and chill them in the fridge for 20 to 30 minutes before baking.

In a small dish, whisk together the egg and water to make the egg wash. Brush the tops of the pies with the egg wash. Sprinkle the tops with flaky sea salt and pepper, if desired. Bake the pies for about 25 minutes, or until the puff pastry is golden brown. Serve the pies hot or enjoy cold at a later time.

To store, keep the pies in an airtight container in the refrigerator for 4 to 5 days.

Makes about 12 pies

1 head of garlic (50 g)

1 tbsp (15 ml) olive oil

1 cup (210 g) cold butternut squash puree

4 oz (113 g) goat cheese

2 tbsp (4 g) fresh thyme leaves

1 tsp kosher sea salt

½ tsp freshly cracked black pepper, plus more for serving

2 sheets (520 g) frozen puff pastry, thawed

1 large egg + 1 tbsp (15 ml) water, for egg wash

Flaky sea salt, for serving, optional

Whimsical Cookies and Bars

In the pages of this whimsical chapter, we will explore the enchanting world of cookies that are anything but ordinary. With a dash of fairy dust and a sprinkle of fresh fruit and flowers, you can transform classic cookies and bars into something truly magical. Inspired by the beauty of folklore and nature, each cookie in this chapter feels as though it was baked by the gentle hands of woodland fair folk.

While cookies have many different names and variations all across the globe, the recipes found here are particularly unique. From waffle cookies to buttery shortbread and fudgy brownies, there is something for every occasion and every palate. Come along on this enchanted cookie journey and create some truly blissful treats!

There are lovely, fresh, and fruity accents like Berry-Filled Pizzelle Cookies (page 51) or Rose-Infused Lemon Bars (page 65). For something a bit richer, there are Mascarpone Espresso Brownies with Peanut Butter Ganache (page 62) and Brown Sugar Shortbread Acorn Cookies (page 58).

Berry-Filled Pizzelle Cookies

Cute, sweet, and perfect for your next garden party, these little pizzelle cookies are shaped into bowls and filled with a deliciously soft almond whipped cream. Your choice of delicious summer berries can be placed on top for a touch of freshness and color. Pizzelles are an Italian waffle cookie flavored with almond extract and cooked until crispy, making them extra crunchy! They can be shaped many ways, like a cannoli or a bowl, or left flat.

Begin by making the Pizzelle Cookies. In a medium bowl, sift together the flour, baking powder, and salt. Set the bowl aside.

In a large bowl, beat the eggs and sugar together with a hand-held electric mixer or whisk until the eggs are pale yellow in color and syrupy, about 4 minutes. They should leave a trace in the batter when the whisk is held above the bowl. Stir in the melted butter, almond extract, and vanilla.

Fold in one half of the dry ingredients until they are no longer visible, then fold in the second half of the dry ingredients. Stir until just combined and no dry ingredients are visible, about 4 minutes.

Heat a pizzelle iron according to the appliance instructions. My pizzelle iron is a newer electric one that makes 2 pizzelles at a time. Spray the iron with cooking spray. Place 2 table-spoons (44 g) of batter per pizzelle on the hot iron and cook for about 1 minute and 30 seconds, or until the pizzelles are a light golden brown and still a bit soft. They need to be soft to be able to shape!

Remove the pizzelles with a spatula and place them on a wire cooling rack. Immediately, while the pizzelles are still hot, place them over the bottom of a half-pint jar or the bottom of a standard muffin tin. If they are too hot for your hands, place a tea towel in between your hands and the pizzelle. Gently shape them over the curve of the glass and hold them until they begin to cool slightly and retain their shape, 2 to 3 minutes.

Place the shaped pizzelles on a wire cooling rack, with the bowl facing upside down. After the pizzelles have cooled to room temperature, 8 to 10 minutes, you can break off any imperfect edges. Repeat with the remaining batter. Let the pizzelles cool fully before filling. The pizzelles can be made ahead of time and kept in an airtight container at room temperature for 3 to 4 days.

(continued)

Makes about 12 cookies

Pizzelle Cookies

1¾ cups (219 g) all-purpose flour

2 tsp (9 g) baking powder

¼ tsp salt

4 large eggs

¾ cup (150 g) granulated sugar

1½ cups (360 ml) melted salted butter

1 tbsp (15 ml) almond extract

1 tsp vanilla extract

Next, make the Almond Whipped Cream Filling. In a large bowl, whip the cream cheese until smooth and fluffy, 2 to 4 minutes. Beat in the sweetened condensed milk, almond extract, salt, and powdered sugar until fully blended into the cream cheese, about 4 minutes. Fold in the whipped cream.

Scoop the cream filling into a piping bag fitted with a large open star tip. If the filling has warmed, place it into the fridge for about 20 minutes. Pipe the cream into the pizzelle cookie bowls. Top the pizzelles with fresh berries of your choice. Dust the little cookie bowls with powdered sugar. Serve the pizzelles chilled.

To store the pizzelles, I recommend separating the components before assembling the tarts. The cookies can be kept at room temperature, wrapped or covered, for about 1 week. The cream filling should be kept in an airtight container in the refrigerator for 4 to 5 days.

Almond Whipped Cream Filling

8 oz (226 g) cream cheese, softened

⅓ cup (80 ml) sweetened condensed milk, chilled

½ tsp almond extract

¼ tsp kosher salt

4 cups (480 g) powdered sugar, sifted

½ cup (120 ml) whipped cream

2 cups (260 g) assorted fresh berries, such as strawberries, blueberries, or blackberries

Powdered sugar, for dusting

Tiramisu Blondies

Have you heard of blondies? Similar to the classic brownie, they omit the chocolate and have a distinct butterscotch flavor. These treats were first introduced by Fannie Farmer in her 1896 cookbook and have since then been adored by many. Imagine, if you will, taking this scrumptious dessert to a whole new level of enchantment by layering the bars with soft, homemade ladyfingers and light, pillowy mascarpone cream. The result is a dessert bar as delicate and airy as a fairy's wings. Let's not forget the finishing touch: a sprinkling of decadent espresso and cocoa powder dusted perfectly on top!

Preheat the oven to 350°F (177°C). Line a large baking sheet with parchment paper and set this aside.

Begin by making the Ladyfingers. In a medium bowl, whip together the egg yolks and ⅓ cup (33 g) of the sugar until they are pale yellow and syrupy, about 4 minutes. Whisk in the salt and vanilla.

In a separate large bowl, beat the egg whites until soft peaks form or the tips curl, 2 to 3 minutes. Gradually add the remaining ⅓ cup (33 g) of sugar to the beaten egg whites, 1 tablespoon (15 ml) at a time, until stiff peaks form or the tips stand straight up. Drizzle the egg yolk mixture into the egg whites and gently fold them in.

In a small bowl, sift together the cake flour and cornstarch. Fold this in gradually to the egg mixture until there are no longer any visible dry bits, 2 to 3 minutes.

Transfer the batter to a piping bag fitted with a large round tip. Pipe the batter onto the baking sheet, making 1 x 3–inch (2.5 x 7.5–cm) logs. Space the ladyfingers about 1 inch (2.5 cm) apart. Dust the tops of the ladyfingers with the powdered sugar. Bake the ladyfingers for 14 to 15 minutes, or until they are lightly golden and crisp. Set the ladyfingers aside to cool on a wire cooling rack, or they can be stored in an airtight container at room temperature for 2 to 3 days.

(continued)

Makes about 12 bars

Ladyfingers

3 egg yolks

⅔ cup (66 g) caster or baker's sugar, divided

Pinch of kosher salt

1 tsp vanilla extract

3 egg whites

1 cup (120 g) cake flour, sifted

2 tbsp (16 g) cornstarch

¼ cup (30 g) powdered sugar, for dusting

With the oven still at 350°F (177°C), begin making the Blondies. Spray a 9 x 13–inch (22 x 33–cm) baking pan and line it with parchment paper, hanging over all of the edges of the pan.

In a large bowl, combine the melted butter with the brown sugar. Whisk in the eggs, one at a time, followed by the vanilla. Stir in the flour, baking powder, and salt until the batter is no longer dry, 2 to 3 minutes. Spread the batter evenly into the prepared baking dish and bake the blondies for 45 to 50 minutes, or until a toothpick inserted in the center comes out clean. Let the blondies cool to room temperature before decorating them.

While the blondies are cooling, make the Tiramisu Cream. Place a small heat-safe bowl over a pot of simmering water, but do not let the bottom of the bowl touch the surface of the water. Whisk together the egg yolks and sugar until they are thick and reach 160°F (71°C), 10 to 15 minutes. Remove the bowl from the heat and let the yolks cool for about 10 minutes.

Whisk in the salt, mascarpone, and vanilla and set the mixture aside. Meanwhile, in a large bowl, whip the heavy cream until it forms stiff peaks, 5 to 6 minutes. Fold in one half of the whipped cream into the egg yolk mixture, then fold in the second half until a pretty blonde-colored cream has come together.

To assemble the Tiramisu Blondies, bring together the lady-fingers, blondies, and cream, as well as the espresso and cocoa powder. Begin by dunking the ladyfingers into the espresso, one at a time, and layering each on top of the surface of the blondies. You may choose to arrange them in any certain way that you wish, but I like a single, symmetrical layer.

Next, evenly spread the Tiramisu Cream over the tops of the lady fingers, all the way to the top edge of the pan. Use a spatula or bench scraper to make the top of the cream as flat as possible. With a fine-mesh sieve, dust the top of the cream with the cocoa powder, completely covering the cream.

Refrigerate the blondies for at least 2 to 3 hours or until the cream has stiffened slightly. Remove the blondies from their pan by pulling out the parchment paper. Slice the blondies into twelve equal-sized squares, squaring off any edges as needed. Serve the blondies chilled with a cup of coffee or espresso!

To store the blondies, keep them covered in the refrigerator for about 5 days.

Blondies

1 cup (240 ml) melted salted butter, slightly cooled

2 cups (388 g) light brown sugar, packed

4 large eggs

2 tsp (10 ml) vanilla extract

2 cups (250 g) all-purpose flour

1 tsp baking powder

1 tsp kosher salt

Tiramisu Cream

6 egg yolks

⅔ cup (133 g) granulated sugar

¼ tsp kosher salt

24 oz (672 g) mascarpone, softened

2 tsp (10 ml) vanilla extract

1½ cups (360 ml) heavy cream

1 tbsp (6 g) Dutch cocoa powder, for dusting

1 cup (240 ml) cold espresso or dark coffee, for dunking

Raspberry and White Chocolate Chunk Cookies

On a beautiful afternoon filled with the fragrance of late spring flowers and the sun peeking through the leaves on the swaying branches, it's the perfect time to whip up a batch of these irresistible Raspberry and White Chocolate Chunk Cookies. The combination of tangy raspberries and creamy white chocolate is a perfect match. Delightfully chewy with crispy edges, these cookies are certain to become a new favorite for any occasion. Whether you are enjoying a picnic in the meadow or cozying up by the wood stove, they will add a touch of sweetness to any moment. Put on your apron and warm up the oven!

In the bowl of a standing electric mixer fitted with a paddle attachment, cream together the butter and brown sugar. Mix in the eggs, one at a time, until fully incorporated, 1 to 2 minutes. Mix in the vanilla, baking soda, and salt.

Add the flour gradually, mixing on low to medium speed until a dough forms, about 2 minutes. Reserve about 1 tablespoon (8 g) of the white chocolate chunks for decorating the cookies. Gently fold in the remaining white chocolate chunks and the raspberries. It is okay if the raspberries break and spread a bit. Be careful to avoid overmixing the dough at this stage.

Press the dough out into a flat disc and wrap it in plastic wrap. Chill the dough for at least 1 hour or overnight. After chilling the dough, let it rest on the countertop for about 20 minutes to soften slightly.

Preheat the oven to 375°F (191°C). Set aside two large baking sheets.

Measure out ¼ cup (84 g) of the dough and shape it into a ball. Flatten the ball slightly on the cookie sheet, making a small disc shape. Repeat with the remaining dough, spacing the cookies about 4 inches (10 cm) apart. Press the reserved white chocolate chunks into the tops of the cookies in a decorative fashion.

Bake the cookies for 15 to 16 minutes, or until the edges are lightly browned and the centers are set. Cool the cookies on the baking sheets for 10 minutes before moving them to a wire cooling rack with a spatula.

These cookies can be stored in an airtight container at room temperature for about 1 week, or they can be frozen and enjoyed at a later date.

Makes about 12 cookies

1 cup (232 g) salted butter, softened

1 cup (194 g) light brown sugar, packed

2 large eggs

2 tsp (10 ml) vanilla extract

½ tsp baking soda

½ tsp kosher salt

2½ cups (312 g) all-purpose flour

1 cup (150 g) white chocolate chunks, divided

1 cup (124 g) fresh raspberries

Brown Sugar Shortbread Acorn Cookies

As if found on the forest floor, these cute little acorn cookies are flavored with brown sugar for a richer base than a classic shortbread. The combination of brown sugar and butter creates a warm and comforting aroma that will fill your kitchen with the cozy vibes of autumn. Dip the tops of the shortbread in melted chocolate and decorate them with chopped nuts. They look almost like real acorns with hairy caps. These cookies are so buttery that they will melt in your mouth and leave you yearning to bake up another batch right away!

In the bowl of a standing electric mixer, cream together the butter and brown sugar until light and fluffy, about 4 minutes. Beat in the vanilla, then add the salt and flour. The dough will start out looking crumbly but will eventually come together as a lightly brown-colored dough ball, 5 to 6 minutes.

Shape the dough into a disc and wrap tightly in plastic wrap. Refrigerate the dough for at least 1 hour.

Preheat the oven to 325°F (163°C). Set aside two large baking sheets.

Shape about 1½ tablespoons (27 g) of dough into a diamond shape, like an acorn. Repeat with the remaining dough and place the cookies about 2 inches (5 cm) apart on the baking sheets. Bake the cookies for 14 to 15 minutes, or until golden brown and set. Let the cookies cool on the baking sheets for about 5 minutes before moving to a wire cooling rack.

Meanwhile, melt the chocolate chips in a double boiler. Dip the tops of the cookies into the chocolate, only coating the front side of the cookie. While the chocolate is still wet, dip the cookies into the assorted chopped nuts of your choice.

Taking the 12 pecan halves that you reserved, slice them in half lengthwise to create a long sliver. Stick these into the melted chocolate to act as the stem of the acorn. Store these cookies at room temperature in an airtight container for 7 or more days.

Makes about 24 cookies

1 cup (232 g) salted butter, softened

½ cup (97 g) light brown sugar, packed

2 tsp (10 ml) vanilla extract

½ tsp kosher salt

2½ cups (312 g) all-purpose flour

2 cups (336 g) chocolate chips

2 cups (195 g) chopped assorted nuts, such as pecans, walnuts, or almonds

12 pecan halves, for decorating

Lemon German Springerle

Springerle are a cookie with a German history, traced back to the German holiday Julfest, a midwinter celebration where the cookies were left as offerings. Made with wooden molds that are either carved by hand or by machine, the cookie dough is pressed into the mold, removed, and then baked, retaining the shape. There are many lovely molds handmade by artists online or in little local shops. While these cookies are traditionally served during the winter holiday, they are wonderful to eat year round, if you have the right mold! I love this sweet little floral bird mold (from my Etsy friend Christmas Cookie House) that pairs beautifully with the lemon flavor of this buttery cookie.

Preheat the oven to 375°F (191°C). Set aside two large ungreased baking sheets.

In the bowl of a standing electric mixer fitted with a paddle attachment, cream the butter, 1 cup (125 g) of the flour, and the sugar until it is light and fluffy, 2 to 4 minutes. Beat in the heavy cream, vanilla, egg yolks, lemon juice, lemon zest, and salt until well combined, another 2 minutes.

Stir in the remaining 2 cups (250 g) of flour until a stiff dough forms, 3 to 4 minutes. When the dough is no longer crumbly, it is ready for shaping.

Generously flour your springerle molds. Press enough dough into the mold to reach the top edge of the design. Firmly tap the mold onto the counter to release the cookie from the mold. Place the molded cookies onto the prepared baking sheet about 2 inches (5 cm) apart. Repeat with the remaining dough until all of the cookies are shaped.

Bake the cookies for 14 to 16 minutes, depending on the size of your molds, or until they are lightly golden brown around the edges and set in the middle. Let the cookies cool on the baking sheets for 5 minutes before moving them to a wire cooling rack.

Store the cookies in an airtight container at room temperature for about 7 or more days.

Makes about 14 cookies

¾ cup (174 g) salted butter, softened

3 cups (375 g) all-purpose flour, divided, plus more for dusting

1 cup (200 g) granulated sugar

2 tbsp (30 ml) heavy cream

½ tsp vanilla extract

2 egg yolks

2 tbsp (30 ml) fresh lemon juice

2 tbsp (15 g) lemon zest

Pinch of kosher salt

Mascarpone Espresso Brownies with Peanut Butter Ganache

Can you smell the scent of chocolate wafting from the oven? In this recipe, indulgent chocolate brownies with a super soft cake-like crumb are topped with a subtly sweet mascarpone frosting and a thin layer of peanut butter ganache. Try sprinkling a little bit of flaky sea salt on top for added flavor and crunch. Don your apron and kerchief for an afternoon of romantically whisking chocolate batter while you listen to birdsong and daydream!

Preheat the oven to 350°F (177°C). Spray an 8 x 8–inch (20 x 20–cm) baking dish with cooking spray and line it with parchment paper, folding it over the sides. For easier use, use clamps to hold down the parchment paper.

To make the Mascarpone Brownies, in a large bowl, whisk together the melted butter, vegetable oil, caster sugar, and brown sugar until the sugar has dissolved slightly, about 2 minutes. Whisk in the beaten eggs and vanilla.

In a medium bowl, whisk together the salt, flour, and cocoa powder. Fold this into the wet ingredients until a thick, syrupy batter forms, about 2 minutes. Fold in the mascarpone until it is incorporated into the batter, another 1 to 2 minutes, and then fold in the chocolate chips.

Pour the batter into the prepared baking dish, spreading it evenly, and bake the brownies for 50 to 60 minutes, or until a toothpick comes out a little crumbly. Let the brownies cool to room temperature in their pan.

While the brownies cool, make the Mascarpone Frosting. In a medium bowl, cream together the mascarpone and butter. Slowly add the powdered sugar, followed by the vanilla and salt, until a soft frosting comes together. It should have the consistency of a traditional buttercream frosting. Spread this over the cooled brownies as evenly as possible. Use a bench scraper or metal spatula to create a level surface. Place the pan of brownies into the fridge while you make the ganache.

(continued)

Makes 9 brownies

Mascarpone Brownies

1 cup (240 ml) melted salted butter, slightly cooled

2 tbsp (30 ml) vegetable oil

1¼ cups (242 g) caster or baker's sugar

1 cup (194 g) light brown sugar, packed

4 large eggs, lightly beaten

1 tbsp (15 ml) vanilla extract

1 tsp kosher salt

1 cup (125 g) all-purpose flour

1 cup (100 g) Dutch cocoa powder

½ cup (116 g) mascarpone, softened

1¼ cups (197 g) semisweet chocolate chips

Mascarpone Frosting

½ cup (116 g) mascarpone, softened

¼ cup (58 g) salted butter, softened

3 cups (354 g) powdered sugar, sifted

2 tsp (10 ml) vanilla extract

Pinch of kosher salt

To make the Peanut Butter Ganache, place a small bowl over a pot of simmering water. The bottom of the bowl should not touch the water. Pour the heavy cream, peanut butter, and white chocolate chips into the bowl. Stir the chocolate and peanut butter into the cream consistently, until the chocolate melts and the mixture turns a lightly colored brown from the melted peanut butter. It is finished when all of the chocolate has melted, 6 to 8 minutes. Remove the bowl from the heat and stir in the vanilla.

Leave the ganache on the countertop for about 10 minutes, stirring it every few minutes, to help it cool down a bit. Pour the slightly cooled ganache over the frosting and spread it evenly. Refrigerate the brownies until the ganache has fully hardened, 6 to 8 hours or overnight.

Once the ganache is hardened, remove the brownies from their pan by lifting out the parchment paper. Slice the brownies into nine slices, fixing any edges that are not smooth after baking. If they are not being served immediately, keep the brownies chilled for up to 5 days.

Peanut Butter Ganache

½ cup (120 ml) heavy cream

¼ cup (60 ml) creamy peanut butter

½ cup (115 g) white chocolate chips

½ tsp vanilla extract

Rose-Infused Lemon Bars

There is something nostalgic about catching the subtle floral scent of roses while walking through the garden. I wanted to capture that essence in a deliciously tart baked good, and these lemons bars turned out to be the perfect pairing. Infused with fresh rose petals and flavored with freshly squeezed lemon juice, you will absolutely love the floral hints that this dessert leaves behind. Wouldn't you love to open your picnic basket with a little lemon bar surprise inside?

Before baking, make the Rose-Infused Sugar. In a blender or food processor, pulse together the sugar and fresh rose petals until the rose petals are finely chopped, about 2 minutes. Make sure to not overly blend and accidentally create powdered sugar. The sugar crystals should be fine with flecks of finely chopped rose petals, and the sugar will be either a light or dark pink, depending on the color of your roses. Rose-Infused Sugar can be kept in an airtight container at room temperature for several weeks.

When you are ready to bake the lemon bars, begin with the Shortcrust. Spray a 9 x 13–inch (22 x 33–cm) baking pan with cooking spray. Line the pan with parchment paper, pressing it to the sides to stick, then set the pan aside.

In a large bowl, whisk together the flour, granulated sugar, powdered sugar, and salt. Cut the cold butter into the dry ingredients with a pastry blender, fork, or your hands until it resembles coarse crumbs about the size of a pea.

Press the crust into the bottom of the prepared baking pan. Do your best to make the crust as even as possible, as it will be crumbly. You can even the layer out with a bench scraper, if necessary. Chill the crust for at least 30 minutes.

Meanwhile, preheat the oven to 350°F (177°C). Bake the chilled crust for 15 minutes, or until it has begun to form into a crust and is a bit wet from the melted butter. Then, let it cool slightly while you make the Lemon Curd.

(continued)

Makes 12 bars

Rose-Infused Sugar

3 cups (600 g) granulated sugar

½ cup (20 g) fresh, food-grade rose petals

Shortcrust

2 cups (250 g) all-purpose flour

¼ cup (50 g) granulated sugar

¼ cup (30 g) powdered sugar

¼ tsp kosher salt

1 cup (232 g) salted butter, cold and cut into ½-inch (1.3-cm) cubes

To make the Lemon Curd, in a large bowl, whisk together the Rose-Infused Sugar and eggs, until the eggs are pale yellow and the sugar has mostly dissolved, about 4 minutes. Whisk in the lemon juice and zest until just combined, about 1 minute more.

In a medium bowl, whisk together the flour, baking powder, and salt. Fold the dry ingredients into the egg mixture until the flour is no longer visible, and there are no lumps in the batter, 1 to 2 minutes.

Pour the Lemon Curd over the par-baked crust. Reduce the oven temperature to 325°F (163°C). Bake the lemon bars for 50 to 60 minutes, or until the center is set and no longer jiggles and the top is a pale brown color.

Place the pan into the refrigerator to chill completely before cutting into bars, about 1 hour. After chilling, lift the bars from the pan using the parchment paper. Dust the top of the bars with powdered sugar and slice into 12 squares or rectangles. Serve chilled with fresh lemon slices as decoration. To store the lemon bars, keep them chilled in an airtight container for about 5 days.

Lemon Curd

3 cups (620 g) Rose-Infused Sugar

8 large eggs

¾ cup (180 ml) fresh lemon juice, about 3 large lemons

4 tsp (10 g) fine lemon zest

½ cup (63 g) all-purpose flour

1 tsp baking powder

¼ tsp kosher salt

½ cup (59 g) powdered sugar, for dusting

Fresh lemon slices, for decorating

Forest Lore Cakes and Icings

For a magical event, you need a truly enchanted cake! This chapter of beautifully decorated cakes was inspired by cozy fantasies—those with deep mystical forests, flowers, and fairies. It's no wonder that forests have captured the imaginations of storytellers and bakers alike for centuries. The lore of the forest is rich and varied, with tales of mischievous fairies, noble woodland creatures, and enchanted plants. What better way to pay homage to the enchanted forest than through the creation of marvelous cakes and dreamy icings inspired by its folklore?

This chapter is filled with the prettiest cakes, like the Pink Lady Strawberry Cake (page 73), Honey and Chamomile Mini Layer Cakes (page 77), and Phases of the Moon Triple Chocolate Cupcakes (page 83). You will also find the heart of the forest in the recipes for the Forest Floor Log Cake (page 71) and the Pistachio Moss Cake Truffles (page 88).

Each treat is made with the most blissful layers of soft cake and rich frostings. You will find all sorts of serving options, like mini cakes or truffles, which are perfect to share with your nearest and dearest. These folklore tales bring about a sense of wonder, and with every bite of sweet cake, I hope that they ignite your tastebuds, as well as transport you to a world of enchantment and wonder.

Forest Floor Log Cake

Enchanting and magical, this log cake looks as if it was naturally found lying on the forest floor! This cake has a beautiful chocolate buttercream frosting with a caramel cream filling and a deliciously soft vanilla sponge cake. You can be as creative as you like with this recipe, creating adorable meringue mushrooms, green cake crumbled to look like moss, and chocolate shavings to imitate curling bark.

Preheat the oven to 375°F (191°C). Spray a 10 x 15–inch (25 x 38–cm) jelly roll pan with cooking spray and set this aside.

To make the Vanilla Sponge Cake, in a small bowl, whisk together the flour and salt and set aside. In a large bowl, beat the egg yolks until they are pale yellow and foamy, about 4 minutes. Whisk in the heavy cream and vanilla. In a separate large bowl, beat the egg whites and cream of tartar together until soft peaks form or the tips curl, 3 to 4 minutes. Slowly add the caster sugar, 1 tablespoon (15 g) at a time, until stiff peaks form or the tips stand straight. This entire process can take anywhere from 5 to 15 minutes depending on the size of your sugar granules.

Once everything is mixed, drizzle half of the egg yolk mixture into the egg whites. Gently fold them together until they are well incorporated, about 2 minutes. Drizzle in the second half of the egg yolk mixture into the egg whites. Fold again, then fold the dry ingredients in. Once the batter has been mixed and it is rather foamy, spread it into the prepared baking pan.

Bake the cake for 15 minutes, or until the top has turned golden brown and it springs back when pressed upon with your fingertip. While the cake is baking, lay out a large tea towel and sprinkle it generously with the powdered sugar.

Immediately invert the cake onto the prepared towel and, taking the short end of the towel, roll the cake up while it is still hot, enclosing the towel in the rolls. Lift the towel up from the ends and place it on a wire cooling rack. Allow the cake to cool until it is still slightly warm but not too cold, 25 to 30 minutes at most. If the cake is too cold, it can crack while you try to unroll it.

While the cake cools, make the Caramel Cream Filling. In a large bowl, whip the heavy cream and powdered sugar together until the cream forms stiff peaks or the peaks stand straight up, 5 to 6 minutes. Gently fold in the caramel sauce until it is well blended into the cream, 1 to 2 minutes.

Carefully unroll the warm cake and spread the filling on top. Roll the cake back up around the cream and refrigerate the cake until ready to frost.

Makes 1 (10-inch [25-cm]) cake

Vanilla Sponge Cake

1 cup (120 g) cake flour, sifted

¼ tsp kosher salt

5 egg yolks

1 tbsp (15 ml) heavy cream

1 tsp vanilla extract

5 egg whites

¼ tsp cream of tartar

1 cup (200 g) caster or baker's sugar

¼ cup (30 g) powdered sugar

Caramel Cream Filling

1 cup (240 ml) heavy cream

¼ cup (30 g) powdered sugar

3 tbsp (45 ml) caramel sauce

(continued)

To make the Chocolate Buttercream Frosting, in a large bowl or standing electric mixer fitted with a paddle attachment, cream the butter for about 2 minutes. Mix in the melted chocolate, milk, and vanilla. Add the powdered sugar, 1 cup (118 g) at a time, until the frosting comes to almost stiff peaks with the tips slightly curling, about 5 minutes.

To decorate the cake, spread the frosting in a thin crumb coat layer all over the sides and the ends of the cake. If you would like for the cake to have a branch, cut off one end of the cake at an angle and place it along the side of the log. Refrigerate the cake after the crumb coat has gone on for 15 to 20 minutes. Then, decorate the cake with the remaining frosting. To make the frosting look like tree bark, you may want to use an icing decorating comb or the tines of a fork. At this point, you can store the cake for a day or two before decorating with additional elements, like the meringue mushrooms.

To make the Meringue Mushrooms, begin by whipping together the egg whites, cream of tartar, and vanilla in a large bowl. Beat the whites until they form soft peaks or the tips curl, 3 to 4 minutes. Begin to add in the sugar, 1 tablespoon (15 g) at a time, waiting for each addition to dissolve before adding the next. The meringue is ready at stiff peaks, when the tips stand straight up on their own, 6 to 8 minutes.

Preheat the oven to 200°F (93°C). Line a large baking sheet with parchment paper and set it aside.

Transfer the meringue to a large piping bag fitted with a large round piping tip. Pipe about 18 mushroom caps, or about 1-inch (2.5-cm) round mounds onto one half of the baking sheet. Then, pipe about 18 mushroom stalks by piping the meringue so that it stands straight up, about 2 inches (5 cm) tall. It is okay if they droop slightly.

Bake the meringues for about 1 hour and 30 minutes. Then, turn off the oven and let them cool to room temperature inside of the oven, about 1 hour more. Remove the meringues from the oven and allow them to continue cooling. Once they are fully cooled, roll them in the cocoa powder.

With a toothpick, core out a small hole in the underside of the mushroom caps. Be careful not to poke all of the way through to the other side. Dip the tips of the mushroom stalks into the melted chocolate. Poke the dipped tips of the stalks into the hole in the bottom of the mushroom caps. Let them cool slightly and then place them on their sides to finish drying.

Decorate the final cake with the meringue mushrooms and shaved chocolate. Store the cake separately from the meringue mushrooms. Keep the cake covered in the refrigerator for about 4 days. To store the meringues, leave them in an airtight container at room temperature for 3 to 4 days.

Chocolate Buttercream Frosting

1 cup (232 g) salted butter, softened

2 oz (57 g) semisweet or dark chocolate, melted

2 tbsp (30 ml) milk

½ tsp vanilla extract

4 cups (472 g) powdered sugar

Meringue Mushrooms

2 egg whites

¼ tsp cream of tartar

½ tsp vanilla extract

½ cup (100 g) caster or baker's sugar

¼ cup (25 g) Dutch cocoa powder

1 oz (30 ml) melted semisweet chocolate chips

Shaved chocolate, for decorating

Pink Lady Strawberry Cake

It's time for a flower fairy tea! This charming Pink Lady Strawberry Cake is just as scrumptious as it is beautiful to look at. Made with real strawberries throughout, the flavor is undeniably fresh and creates the loveliest shade of soft pink. This cake is decorated in a vintage Lambeth style, but you may choose to decorate your perfect pink lady cake any way that you like. Lambeth cakes are renowned for being ruffly and perfectly sweet, with their delicate piping details, making this cake the ideal romantic treat for your next party.

Begin by making the Strawberry Reduction. In a medium saucepan, combine the strawberries, sugar, lemon juice, lemon zest, and salt. Stir over medium-high heat, bringing the mixture to a boil. Lower the heat and reduce the jam to a simmer. Continue to cook and stir the fruit mixture until thickened and reduced by half, about 15 minutes. You will want to end up with about 1 cup (240 ml) of reduction. Remove the pan from the heat and let the reduction cool to room temperature. To speed up this process, you may place it into the refrigerator covered with plastic wrap, stirring every 10 minutes. Once the reduction has cooled, reserve about ¼ cup (60 ml) from the rest. You will use this for filling between the cake layers.

Preheat the oven to 350°F (177°C). Grease and flour three 9-inch (23-cm) cake pans and set them aside while you make the Strawberry Cake batter.

In a medium bowl, sift together the flour, baking powder, baking soda, and salt. Set this aside. In the bowl of a standing electric mixer fitted with a paddle attachment, cream together the butter and sugar until it is pale yellow and fluffy, 3 to 4 minutes. Add in the egg whites, one at a time, waiting until each white is fully incorporated into the batter before adding the next, about 10 minutes total. This creates a light and airy cake. Mix in the vanilla and strawberry extract.

Begin to add the flour mixture and buttermilk, alternately, beginning and ending with the flour mixture. Once these have been added, fold in ½ cup (120 ml) of the Strawberry Reduction. Stir the cake until just combined, 1 to 2 minutes.

Divide the batter between the cake pans. Tap the pans on the countertop to remove any large air bubbles. Bake the cakes in the center rack for 30 to 35 minutes, or until a toothpick inserted in the center comes out clean. Let the cakes cool in their pans for about 10 minutes before removing them to a wire cooling rack. Let the cakes cool to room temperature before decorating.

(continued)

Makes 1 (9-inch [23-cm]) 3-layer cake

Strawberry Reduction

32 oz (896 g) fresh strawberries, quartered

½ cup (100 g) granulated sugar

1 tbsp (15 ml) fresh lemon juice

1 tsp lemon zest

Pinch of kosher salt

Strawberry Cake

3 cups (360 g) cake flour, sifted

1½ tsp (7 g) baking powder

1 tsp baking soda

½ tsp kosher salt

1½ cups (348 g) salted butter, softened

2 cups (400 g) granulated sugar

6 egg whites, room temperature

2 tsp (10 ml) vanilla extract

1 tsp strawberry extract

¾ cup (180 ml) buttermilk, room temperature

½ cup (120 ml) Strawberry Reduction

Meanwhile, make the Pink Lady Buttercream Frosting. In a large bowl or standing electric mixer fitted with a paddle attachment, cream the butter until smooth, about 1 minute. Beat in the remaining ¼ cup (60 ml) of Strawberry Reduction, vanilla, and salt. Gradually add the powdered sugar until a soft frosting, with somewhat stiff peaks with a curl on the end, forms, about 5 minutes on medium-high speed. If you would prefer to have white icing for the decorating details, reserve some of the frosting before adding the Strawberry Reduction.

Divide the frosting among piping bags if you are decorating the cake in a vintage Lambeth style. I personally used five different piping bags and tips for my cake, but feel free to get creative here and make it your own! Otherwise, set aside.

To assemble the cake, even out the cake layers by slicing off the domes on top of the cakes with a serrated knife so that they lay flat and are all about the same size. Spread a bit of frosting on a plate or cake stand and lay the first cake topside down on the frosting to prevent it from sliding around. Spread frosting on top of the cake layer and then spread about 2 tablespoons (30 ml) of the reserved Strawberry Reduction over the frosting. Layer the next cake on top and repeat the process, followed by the final cake layer. Spread frosting over the top cake layer and all down the sides. You may want to spread two layers of frosting, one as a thin crumb coat and the second as a final layer. Refrigerate the cake for about 10 minutes in between frosting layers to prevent uneven spreading.

To make a Lambeth cake, you will want the sides of the cake as smooth as possible. It is helpful to use a bench scraper, turning the cake as you scrape the frosting smooth. Refrigerate the cake for at least 10 minutes before piping on extra frosting.

To decorate the cake with piped frosting, practice making designs with different tips for fun shapes that you may want. Traditionally, a vintage cake would use different piping tips, such as an open star tip, closed star tip, round tip, drop flower tip, leaf tip, and petal tip.

Top your final cake with fresh strawberries so that each slice receives a piece of fruit. Serve the cake chilled or at room temperature. This cake should be kept in the refrigerator for 4 to 5 days and it freezes beautifully!

Pink Lady Buttercream Frosting

1 cup (232 g) salted butter, softened

¼ cup (60 ml) Strawberry Reduction

1 tsp vanilla extract

Pinch of kosher salt

5 cups (590 g) powdered sugar, sifted

About 8 whole strawberries, for decorating

Tip

For perfect slices, wash your knife in between cuts. To save time, the components of this cake can be made ahead of time and assembled at a later date for less work!

Honey and Chamomile Mini Layer Cakes

Summertime is marked by the blossoming of sweet chamomile flowers and the honeybees buzzing from bloom to bloom. What better way to celebrate the season than with these enchanting miniature sponge cakes? Layered with a syrupy honey butterscotch glaze and topped with creamy chamomile-infused cream cheese frosting, they are the perfect addition to any garden party. Crafting these treats is easy and you will finish with a collection of irresistibly pretty cakes that are simply charming. Set them at each place setting for the most darling of gatherings underneath a canopy of blossoms.

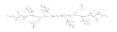

Begin by making the Sponge Cake. Preheat the oven to 350°F (177°C). Grease and flour a 9 x 13–inch (22 x 33–cm) cake pan and set this aside.

In a medium bowl, sift together the flour, baking powder, and salt. Set this aside. In a large bowl, beat the egg yolks for 3 minutes, or until they are foamy. Beat in the sugar, 1 tablespoon (15 g) at a time, until the eggs become pale in color and syrupy in consistency, about 4 minutes. Fold the dry ingredients into the egg mixture until just combined, about 2 minutes.

After the eggs are beaten, place the milk and butter in a small saucepan over the stove. Warm the milk and butter over medium-low heat until it reaches 120°F (49°C), or it just begins to bubble around the edges of the pan, 6 to 8 minutes. Immediately pour the hot milk and butter into the batter. Stir the milk mixture into the batter with a wooden spoon or spatula until everything is smooth, 2 to 3 minutes.

Pour the batter into the prepared cake pan and bake the cake for 25 to 30 minutes, or until the top of the cake is golden brown and springs back when pressed upon. You can also test the cake with a toothpick, and it should come out a bit crumbly but not soupy. Let the cake rest for about 10 minutes in the pan before inverting it onto a wire cooling rack to finish cooling.

(continued)

Makes 6 (3-inch [8-cm]) 2-layer mini cakes

Sponge Cake

2 cups (250 g) cake flour, sifted

4 tsp (18 g) baking powder

½ tsp kosher salt

4 egg yolks

2 cups (400 g) granulated sugar

1 cup (240 ml) whole milk

¼ cup (58 g) salted butter

Meanwhile, begin making the Chamomile Cream Cheese Frosting. To a small saucepan, add the heavy cream and dried chamomile flowers. Warm the cream with the chamomile until the cream reaches about 110°F (43°C), or it just begins to bubble around the edges of the pan, about 2 to 3 minutes. Turn off the heat and let the chamomile steep in the cream for about 30 minutes. Over a small bowl, strain the infused cream through a fine-mesh sieve and reserve it.

In a large bowl or standing electric mixer fitted with a paddle attachment, cream together the cream cheese and butter. Add the vanilla and salt, then slowly incorporate the powdered sugar until the frosting begins to come together. Beat in the chamomile-infused cream and beat the frosting until it comes to stiff peaks, 2 to 4 minutes. Scoop the frosting into a piping bag fitted with a closed star tip and set it aside until ready to use.

To make the Honey Butterscotch Glaze, add the sugar, honey, heavy cream, butter, and salt to a small saucepan. Warm the ingredients over medium heat and bring them to a boil, stirring consistently to prevent scorching. Continue to cook and stir until the sugar dissolves, about 10 minutes. It will become bubbly, similar to cooking caramel candy. Remove the pan from the heat and let the glaze cool to room temperature.

When you are ready to assemble the cakes, cut the Sponge Cake into circles with a 3-inch (8-cm) biscuit cutter. You will end up with about 12 cake layers. To assemble the cakes, pipe frosting onto one layer of cake. Then spread the Honey Butterscotch Glaze over the frosting. Top with a second layer of cake. Pipe on more frosting and drizzle with the glaze. Decorate the top with fresh chamomile flowers. Repeat with the remaining cakes. Store the cakes at room temperature or in the refrigerator until ready to serve, about 4 days.

Chamomile Cream Cheese Frosting

¼ cup (60 ml) heavy cream

2 tbsp (4 g) dried chamomile flowers

4 oz (113 g) cream cheese, softened

¼ cup (58 g) salted butter, softened

2 tsp (10 ml) vanilla extract

Pinch of kosher salt

4 cups (472 g) powdered sugar, sifted

Honey Butterscotch Glaze

⅓ cup (66 g) granulated sugar

¼ cup (60 ml) honey

½ cup (120 ml) heavy cream

1 tbsp (14 g) salted butter

Pinch of kosher salt

Fresh chamomile flowers, for decorating

Lavender and Earl Grey Petit Fours

Earl Grey is a classic British tea made from a Ceylon black tea base and flavored with the rinds of bergamot oranges. This makes Earl Grey the perfect tea to pair with cream and sugar. In this case, it partners utterly well with a spongey cake flavored with lavender buds. Petit fours, while often thought of as difficult, are simply a large sheet cake cut into small squares and dipped in melted chocolate or fondant! You will love these mini fairy cakes for a sweet gathering. Decorate each little cake with a dot of lavender buttercream and dried lavender buds for a touch of whimsy.

Begin by making the Lavender Earl Grey Cake. In a small saucepan over medium-low heat, warm the buttermilk until it just starts to simmer around the edges of the pan, about 2 minutes. Remove the pan from the heat and drop in the loose-leaf Earl Grey tea and lavender buds. Cover the pan with a lid and let it steep for 10 to 15 minutes. Strain the buttermilk through a fine-mesh sieve over a bowl. Let the infused buttermilk come to room temperature, 15 to 20 minutes.

Preheat the oven to 350°F (177°C). Grease and flour a 9 x 13–inch (22 x 33–cm) cake pan and set this aside.

In a medium bowl, sift together the flour, baking powder, baking soda, salt, and finely ground Earl Grey tea leaves. Set this aside.

In the bowl of a standing electric mixer fitted with a paddle attachment, cream the butter and sugar together until the butter is pale yellow and fluffy, 3 to 4 minutes. Add in the eggs, incorporating each fully before adding the next, another 6 to 8 minutes total. Then mix in the vanilla. Alternately, begin to add the flour mixture and the infused buttermilk, beginning and ending with the flour mixture until the cake batter is thick and smooth, 5 to 6 minutes.

Pour the batter into the prepared baking pan and tap the pan lightly on the countertop to remove any large air bubbles. Bake the cake for 30 to 35 minutes, or until a toothpick inserted in the center comes out clean. Let the cake rest in the pan for about 10 minutes before inverting it onto a wire cooling rack to finish cooling to room temperature.

While the cake is cooling, make the Lavender Buttercream Frosting. In the same small saucepan that you infused the buttermilk, warm the milk over medium heat to almost simmering. Remove the pan from the heat and drop in the lavender buds. Cover the pan and let the milk infuse for 10 to 15 minutes. In a similar fashion as before, strain the milk and reserve it for use in the frosting. Let the milk cool to room temperature before mixing.

Makes about 30 (2-inch [5-cm]) petit fours

Lavender Earl Grey Cake

1 cup (240 ml) buttermilk, room temperature

1 tbsp (5 g) loose-leaf Earl Grey tea

1 tbsp (6 g) dried culinary lavender buds

3 cups (360 g) cake flour

1½ tsp (7 g) baking powder

1 tsp baking soda

½ tsp kosher salt

1 tsp finely ground Earl Grey tea leaves

1 cup (232 g) salted butter, softened

2 cups (400 g) granulated sugar

4 large eggs, room temperature

1 tbsp (15 ml) vanilla extract

Lavender Buttercream Frosting

1 cup (240 ml) milk

1 tbsp (6 g) dried culinary lavender buds

(continued)

In the bowl of a standing electric mixer fitted with a paddle attachment, cream together the butter, powdered sugar, vanilla, salt, and lavender-infused milk until fully combined. Add any food coloring, if desired. Reserve about ¼ cup (60 g) of frosting for decorating the tops of the petit fours.

To assemble the petit fours, slice the sheet cake in half crosswise with a serrated knife. Then cut each cake square into a bottom and top half, slicing horizontally through the center. You should have four pieces. Open the cake so that the inside is revealed. Spread the frosting evenly on two pieces of the open cakes and then sandwich the cakes together. Place the sandwiched cakes on a baking sheet and pop them into the freezer for about 30 minutes.

After the cakes have chilled in the freezer, bring them back out onto the counter and, with a serrated knife, slice them into 2-inch (5-cm) cubes. Place the little cakes back into the freezer for another 20 to 30 minutes.

Next, make the White Chocolate Coating. In a small bowl set over a pot of simmering water, melt the white chocolate and coconut oil, stirring constantly. Whisk in any food coloring that you may want to use. Remove the bowl from the heat and place it onto the countertop.

Using a fork, stab the tops of the petit fours. Dip them into the melted chocolate coating and cover all of the sides. You may choose to use a spoon to help drag any chocolate over difficult-to-reach spots. Lift the dipped cake over the chocolate and allow any excess to drip off back into the pan. If your chocolate begins to harden, you may warm it back up over the pot of simmering water.

Place the dipped cakes onto a wire cooling rack placed over a baking sheet lined with parchment paper to catch any drips. This is easier said than done and will take a bit of practice to figure out how to maneuver the cakes off of the fork tines. Usually another fork is needed!

Let the white chocolate coating harden completely. You may choose to pop the petit fours into the fridge to speed up this process, but it usually takes only about 10 minutes, depending on the temperature of your cake and the room.

Once the cakes have hardened, remove them carefully from the wire cooling rack onto a serving plate. Decorate the tops of the petit fours with the reserved buttercream frosting, using a piping bag and decorative piping tip. Sprinkle the tops with some dried lavender buds for playfulness!

To store the petit fours, they can be left at room temperature in an airtight container for about 5 days.

1 cup (232 g) salted butter, softened

4 cups (472 g) powdered sugar, sifted

½ tsp vanilla extract

Pinch of kosher salt

2 drops violet food coloring, optional

White Chocolate Coating

12 oz (336 g) white coating chocolate

2 tbsp (30 ml) coconut oil

2 to 4 drops violet food coloring, optional

Culinary lavender buds, for decorating

Phases of the Moon Triple Chocolate Cupcakes

The phases of the moon hold a special significance to those who are nurturers of the natural world. From the silvery glow of a full moon to the mesmerizing beauty of the new moon, each phase is a declaration to the wonder of nature. Under the light of the full moon, you'll fall in love with this absolute chocolate dream of a cupcake. Soft, spongy chocolate cake is filled with a fluffy dark chocolate mousse and topped with the prettiest satiny mocha buttercream frosting. What truly sets these cupcakes apart is their enchanting decoration—a tribute to the phases of the moon, made with chocolate and vanilla sprinkles. Enjoy the celestial beauty with each decadent chocolate bite!

Begin by making the Dark Chocolate Mousse. Warm the cream and chocolate chips together in a medium saucepan over medium-low heat, stirring until the chocolate melts, 5 to 6 minutes. Be careful not to boil the cream.

Meanwhile, whisk together the egg yolks and sugar until they become pale yellow and syrupy, about 4 minutes. Once the chocolate has fully melted and combined with the cream, pour about 2 tablespoons (30 ml) of the warm cream into the egg yolk mixture, whisking quickly to temper the eggs. Then, pour the entire egg mixture into the pan of cream and chocolate. Whisk in the salt.

Cook the mousse over medium-low heat at barely a simmer until it begins to thicken and coats the back of a spoon, 6 to 8 minutes. Remove the pan from the heat. Cover the mousse with plastic wrap touching its surface and place it into the refrigerator. Stir the mousse every 10 minutes, until it has fully chilled, about 1 hour total. Transfer the mousse to a piping bag and leave in the refrigerator until ready to use.

Preheat the oven to 425°F (218°C). Line a standard 12-cup muffin tin with cupcake liners or lightly grease the muffin cups. Set this aside while you make the cake.

To make the Chocolate Cake, in a large bowl, combine the flour, cocoa powder, sugar, baking powder, salt, and baking soda. To this mixture, whisk in the eggs, vanilla, vegetable oil, buttermilk, and hot coffee until the batter is smooth, 8 to 10 minutes total.

Divide the cupcake batter evenly amongst the muffin cups, filling them about two-thirds of the way full. Bake the cupcakes for 15 minutes. Then, lower the oven temperature to 350°F (177°C) and bake for another 10 to 15 minutes, or until a toothpick inserted in the center of the cupcakes comes out clean. Let the cupcakes rest in the pan for 10 minutes before moving them to a wire cooling rack. Let the cupcakes cool completely before decorating.

Makes about 16 cupcakes

Dark Chocolate Mousse

1 cup (240 ml) heavy cream, divided

½ cup (75 g) dark chocolate chips

2 egg yolks

2 tbsp (25 g) granulated sugar

Pinch of kosher salt

Chocolate Cake

1¼ cups (150 g) cake flour, sifted

6 tbsp (38 g) Dutch cocoa powder

1 cup (200 g) granulated sugar

1½ tsp (7 g) baking powder

½ tsp kosher salt

¼ tsp baking soda

2 large eggs, room temperature

1 tsp vanilla extract

¼ cup (60 ml) vegetable oil

½ cup (120 ml) buttermilk, room temperature

2 tbsp (30 ml) hot black coffee

(continued)

While the cupcakes bake and cool, make the Mocha Buttercream Frosting. Sift together the powdered sugar, cocoa powder, and instant espresso powder. In a separate large bowl, cream together the butter, vanilla, and heavy cream. Stir in the powdered sugar mixture until a thick, glossy frosting comes together with stiff peaks that curl slightly at the ends, about 5 minutes. Transfer the frosting to a piping bag fitted with a star tip.

Finally, assemble the cupcakes. With the wide end of a large piping tip, core out the center of the cupcakes. Discard this center or save it to enjoy later. With the piping bag of mousse, fill all of the cupcakes so that they are at level with the tops of the cupcakes.

Pipe the frosting onto the tops of the cupcakes. Decorate the cupcakes with mocha frosting or piped chocolate designs. To make chocolate designs, simply fill a piping bag with melted chocolate and pipe the designs onto a piece of parchment or wax paper. Let them harden and use as desired. As a final touch, you can sprinkle the edges of the cupcakes with coarse sugar, if you'd like.

Store the cupcakes at room temperature, covered, for 3 to 4 days.

Mocha Buttercream Frosting

4 cups (472 g) powdered sugar

3 tbsp (19 g) Dutch cocoa powder

1½ tsp (2 g) instant espresso powder

½ cup (116 g) salted butter, softened

1 tsp vanilla extract

⅓ cup (80 ml) heavy cream

½ cup (84 g) white chocolate chips, melted, for decoration, optional

½ cup (84 g) semisweet chocolate chips, melted, for decoration, optional

2 tbsp (30 g) coarse sugar, for sprinkling, optional

Painted Marble Spice Cake

This stunning creation is a true work of art. The rich flavors of warm spices like cinnamon, nutmeg, cloves, and ginger are combined with the elegant beauty of marbled cake layers. But what truly sets this cake apart from the rest is the exquisite decoration: a masterpiece of buttercream brushstrokes and floral accents. These intricate details are made with piping bags and tips, as well as some artist's tools like a palette knife and paintbrushes. This cake is the perfect place to let your creativity soar, though it is also a delicious recipe if you prefer to keep your decorations on the more subtle side. Whether enjoyed on a lazy afternoon in the garden or as the centerpiece for a fancy gathering, this cake is sure to delight all who taste it.

Preheat the oven to 350°F (177°C). Grease and flour two 8-inch (20-cm) round cake pans. Set these aside.

To make the Marble Spice Cake, in a large bowl, sift together the cake flour, baking powder, baking soda, and salt. Set this aside. In the bowl of a standing electric mixer fitted with a paddle attachment, cream together the butter and brown sugar until it is light and fluffy, 2 to 4 minutes. Add in the egg whites, one at a time, fully incorporating each into the butter before adding the next, 8 to 10 minutes total. Stir in the vanilla.

In a small dish, whisk together the buttermilk and sour cream. Alternately, begin adding the flour mixture and buttermilk mixture, beginning and ending with the flour mixture. Stir until the batter is just combined, 3 to 4 minutes.

Divide the batter into halves, placing one half in a large bowl and setting it aside. To the batter left in the mixer, add the molasses, cinnamon, cardamom, ginger, nutmeg, and cloves.

With two ¼-cup (60-ml) scoops, begin scooping dollops of each colored cake batter into the prepared pans, layering the two batters on top of each other in concentric circles. Continue this process until all of the batter is used up.

Bake the cakes for 40 to 45 minutes, or until a toothpick inserted in the center comes out clean. Let the cakes rest in their pans for about 10 minutes before inverting them onto a wire cooling rack. Allow the cakes to cool to room temperature before decorating with the frosting.

(continued)

Makes 1 (8-inch [23-cm]) 3-layer cake

Marble Spice Cake

3 cups (360 g) cake flour, sifted

1½ tsp (7 g) baking powder

1 tsp baking soda

½ tsp kosher salt

1½ cups (348 g) salted butter, softened

2 cups (388 g) light brown sugar, packed

6 egg whites, room temperature

1 tbsp (15 ml) vanilla extract

¾ cup (180 ml) buttermilk, room temperature

½ cup (120 ml) sour cream, room temperature

¼ cup (60 ml) molasses

2 tbsp (16 g) ground cinnamon

1 tsp ground cardamom

1 tsp ground ginger

½ tsp ground nutmeg

¼ tsp ground cloves

To make the Vanilla Buttercream Frosting, cream together the butter, vanilla, and heavy cream in a large bowl until the butter is smooth, 2 to 4 minutes. Slowly add the powdered sugar, 1 cup (118 g) at a time, until the frosting reaches a consistency with almost stiff peaks or the tips curl slightly but retain their shape, 4 to 5 minutes. This frosting should be smooth and glossy, so the butter needs to be very soft.

To frost the cake, spread frosting in between the layers. Then spread frosting all across the top of the cake and down the sides in a thin layer to create a crumb coat. Refrigerate the cake for 20 to 30 minutes before applying the next layer of frosting. To create a perfectly smooth edge to the cake, use a bench scraper to scrape off any lumpy frosting. If you are "painting" your cake, use any leftover frosting to create flowers with food coloring of your choice!

To create a painted cake, you will want to divide your buttercream frosting into sections. The majority of the frosting will be used to frost the entire outside of the cake, while the rest will be used to create a design, such as flowers or other botanical elements. Divide the frosting into small amounts and use different food colorings to create various shades.

The painting, or rather heavy layering, is best done with an artist's palette knife. Paint brushes that are only used for food can also be used! Make sure that your cake is fully frosted and has been chilled well. This will make it easier to apply the frosting designs. Try practicing your flowers on a flat surface first, such as a piece of parchment paper. To help with applying the flower petals, make sure that your buttercream is soft and glossy looking, rather than at a crusting stage. If the frosting becomes too soft while decorating, pop the cake back into the fridge for 20 to 30 minutes before continuing to decorate.

To store the cake, keep it in the refrigerator for 4 to 5 days.

Vanilla Buttercream Frosting

1 cup (232 g) salted butter, softened

1 tsp vanilla extract

2 tbsp (30 ml) heavy cream

4 cups (472 g) powdered sugar, sifted

Food coloring, optional

Pistachio Moss Cake Truffles

Have you seen anything as cute as a cake truffle transformed into a little moss ball? It is as if they were left behind by little fairy bakers. As you wander underneath the canopy of the trees, perhaps you might stumble upon one of these delightful little balls of sweet pistachio cake! These truffles are sweetly fashioned with crumbled pistachios to look like moss with pistachio cake and dreamy cream cheese frosting.

Preheat the oven to 350°F (177°C). Grease and flour a 9 x 9–inch (22 x 22–cm) cake pan. Set this aside while you make the Pistachio Cake.

In a large bowl, sift together the flour, baking powder, baking soda, and salt. In the bowl of a standing electric mixer fitted with a paddle attachment, cream together the butter and sugar until it becomes light and fluffy, 3 to 4 minutes. Add in the egg whites, about one at a time, fully incorporating them into the butter before adding the next, 5 to 6 minutes total. Stir in the vanilla and almond extract.

In a small dish, whisk together the buttermilk and sour cream. Alternately, begin adding the flour mixture and buttermilk mixture, beginning and ending with the flour mixture. Stir until the batter is just combined, 3 to 4 minutes. Fold in the ground pistachios until they are well dispersed throughout the batter, 1 minute.

Spread the cake batter evenly into the prepared pan. Bake the cake for 30 to 35 minutes, or until a toothpick inserted in the center comes out clean. Let the cake rest for about 10 minutes in the pan before inverting it onto a wire cooling rack. Let the cake come to room temperature before decorating.

Meanwhile, make the Cream Cheese Frosting. In the bowl of a standing electric mixer fitted with a paddle attachment, cream together the cream cheese, vanilla, almond extract, milk, and salt. Stir in the powdered sugar until the frosting comes to stiff peaks that slightly curl at the end, 3 to 4 minutes. Mix in any green food coloring, if desired.

Once the cake has fully cooled, crumble it into tiny pieces in a large bowl, about the size of a pea. Add the Cream Cheese Frosting and mix the cake and frosting together with your hands, evenly mixing them together. The final result should be a somewhat sticky cake that is like working with play sand. With a spoon or cookie scoop, place about 2 tablespoons (6 g) worth of cake onto a large baking sheet. Repeat with the remaining truffle mixture until all of it has been used. Place the cake truffles into the freezer for about 30 minutes.

Makes about 36 truffles

Pistachio Cake

1½ cups (180 g) cake flour

¾ tsp baking powder

½ tsp baking soda

¼ tsp kosher salt

¾ cup (58 g) salted butter, softened

1 cup (200 g) granulated sugar

3 egg whites, room temperature

1 tsp vanilla extract

1 tsp almond extract

1 cup (240 ml) buttermilk, room temperature

½ cup (120 ml) sour cream, room temperature

1 cup (100 g) ground pistachios

Cream Cheese Frosting

4 oz (113 g) cream cheese, softened

½ tsp vanilla extract

½ tsp almond extract

1 tbsp (15 ml) milk

Pinch of kosher salt

4 cups (472 g) powdered sugar, sifted

Green food coloring, optional

While the truffles are chilling, make the White Chocolate Coating. Bring a small saucepan of water to a simmer. Place a heat-safe bowl over the simmering water. To the bowl, add the white chocolate chips and coconut oil. Stir the chocolate and oil together until the chocolate is fully melted, 6 to 8 minutes. Stir in any green food coloring, if using.

Once the White Chocolate Coating has been made, bring out the cake truffles. With a fork, dip the cake truffles into the coating. Roll the truffles in the ground pistachios. Let the truffles dry on a piece of parchment paper until the chocolate has fully hardened. The truffles can be stored in the refrigerator for about 5 days or frozen to be enjoyed later.

White Chocolate Coating

2 cups (300 g) white chocolate chips

¼ cup (60 ml) coconut oil

Green food coloring, optional

1 cup (100 g) ground pistachios, for rolling

Cozy Hearth Yeast Breads

Bread is a love language. As some of us may decide to follow a life that is simpler and slower-paced, bread tends to be one of the first places we look to make a change in our daily habits. Bread was one of the first foods that I learned how to make from scratch, and it changed everything about how I cooked. There is really nothing quite as lovely as freshly made bread! Whether this is your first attempt at baking a loaf or the hundredth, I hope that is chapter can inspire you to feel the warmth and coziness that is baking from a hearth.

Step back in time with the homey loaves and buns in this chapter. Inside you will find traditional recipes like Pain d'Epi (page 107), Summer Garden Sourdough Focaccia (page 93), and Cottage Sandwich Bread with Variations (page 113). For sweeter breads, you will love the Rolled Brioche Bread (page 99) and Cinnamon Star Bread with Eggnog Icing (page 101). With each fluffy bite, I hope that you are transported to a little cottage in the woods with a cozy fire crackling nearby and the scent of delicious yeasted bread in the air.

Summer Garden Sourdough Focaccia

Imagine waking up in the morning with a beautiful, bubbly sourdough loaf ready to bake as the sun shines brightly on your little kitchen garden outside. Focaccia has a similar flavor to pizza dough, though with a much wetter dough that is roughly shaped and left to rise in its baking pan overnight. In the morning, drizzle the top with olive oil and press in little divots with your fingertips to create a crispy crust. Have fun creating designs to top your loaf with fresh Roma tomatoes, garlic, peppers, and basil leaves from the farmers' market.

Begin by making this bread in the evening with an active sourdough starter. In a large bowl, whisk together the warm water, sourdough starter, 1 tablespoon (15 ml) of the olive oil, and 1½ teaspoons (3 g) of the salt with a fork or bread whisk. Add in the flour and mix together until a thick, sticky dough forms, 3 to 4 minutes. I find this is easiest to do with a bread whisk or a fork, but your hands can work great, too. The dough should be wetter than most bread doughs, but not so wet that it is soupy, and you should still be able to turn it over in your hands. If necessary, add a bit more flour as needed.

Leave the dough in the bowl and cover the bowl with a damp kitchen towel or plastic wrap. Let the dough rest for about 30 minutes. After the resting period, stretch the dough by pulling at the corners and stretching away without breaking the dough. Fold the dough over itself. Repeat this until the dough is shaped into a nice, smooth ball, about two more times around the edge of the bowl.

Grease a 9 x 9–inch (22 x 22–cm) pan. Press the dough into the pan as evenly as possible. Cover the pan with a damp kitchen towel or plastic wrap and let the dough rise on the counter overnight, 8 to 12 hours.

In the morning, slice up the tomato about ⅛ inch (3 mm) thick. Prepare one to two wire cooling racks and cover them with paper towels. Lay the tomato slices on the paper towels and sprinkle them with the remaining 1 teaspoon of salt. Let them sweat for about 30 minutes. Pat them dry with more paper towels.

(continued)

Makes 1 loaf

1⅓ cups (320 ml) warm water

½ cup (133 g) active sourdough starter

2 tbsp (30 ml) extra virgin olive oil, divided

2½ tsp (9 g) kosher salt, divided

3½ cups (438 g) all-purpose flour, plus more for dusting

1 medium Roma tomato (60 g)

Preheat the oven to 425°F (218°C).

Drizzle the top of the dough with the remaining tablespoon (15 ml) of olive oil. With the tips of your fingers, press divots into the top of the dough all over. Let the olive oil roll into the divots. Arrange the tomato slices, sweet peppers, sliced shallot, minced garlic, fresh basil leaves, and fresh thyme over the top of the bread. You may choose to spread them evenly or create a cute design. I love making a garden scene on my focaccia loaves! Sprinkle the cracked pepper and flaky sea salt over the top of the dough.

Bake the focaccia for 40 to 45 minutes, or until the top of the bread is a deep golden brown. Remove it from the pan and serve immediately while it is still hot, with homemade butter or seasoned olive oil.

Store the bread at room temperature wrapped in plastic or a cloth bread bag for about 1 week.

3 small sweet peppers (60 g), seeds removed and sliced into rings

1 shallot (50 g), sliced

3 cloves garlic (12 g), minced

¼ cup (6 g) fresh, whole basil leaves

2 tbsp (4 g) fresh thyme leaves

1 tsp freshly cracked pepper, plus more for serving

1 tsp flaky sea salt, plus more for serving

Homemade butter or seasoned olive oil, for serving

Chive and Asiago Sourdough Boule

There is nothing quite as comforting as a freshly made loaf of sourdough bread. This is my absolute favorite base recipe for making an easy sourdough boule with the addition of fresh herbs like chives and parsley and sharply flavored cheeses. The flavor combination makes this sourdough feel as if it had sprung straight up from your garden beds. It also makes a wonderful base for a grilled cheese sandwich.

In a large bowl, whisk together the warm water, salt, and sourdough starter until the starter breaks down a bit and is almost fully mixed into the water, about 2 minutes.

Add in the flour and stir together the bread with either a fork or a bread whisk. After 2 to 3 minutes, the dough will begin to come together. Once the dough is no longer dry and crumbly and has formed a soft, sticky, and stretchy dough, then it is ready for the resting period. The dough may not look like a quick rising yeast bread's dough; it will be less compact and resemble something closer to a muffin dough.

Cover the bowl with plastic wrap or a damp tea towel and let the dough rest for 30 minutes.

Begin the stretching and pulling process, keeping the dough in the bowl. With wet hands, stretch the dough from one corner, pulling it outwards without breaking it. Fold this back over the center of the dough. Repeat this stretching and pulling around all sides of the dough, rotating the bowl as you go. Tuck the stretched ends underneath the loaf, pulling it toward you slightly to tighten the ball. Cover the bowl again and let the dough rest for 15 minutes. Repeat this stretching and folding process two more times. By the end, your dough should be smoother and less shaggy, representing a more traditional-looking bread dough.

After the final stretching and folding, leave the dough, covered, to sit on the counter for 8 to 12 hours or overnight. If you need more time, simply place the dough into the refrigerator for at least 8 hours or up to 24 hours.

(continued)

Makes 1 loaf

1¾ cups (420 ml) warm water

2 tsp (12 g) kosher salt

1 cup (266 g) active sourdough starter

5 cups (625 g) all-purpose flour, plus more for dusting

In the morning, prepare a bread banneton or a proofing basket lined with a floured kitchen towel. Deflate the dough with your hands and bring it out onto a lightly floured work surface. If you refrigerated the dough overnight, you may want to let it rest at room temperature for about 30 minutes before working with it.

Press the dough out with your hands into a rough rectangle shape, about 6 x 8 inches (15 x 20 cm). Sprinkle the top of the flattened dough with the chives, parsley, about half of the asiago cheese, and about half of the cheddar cheese. Fold the loaf into thirds, like a business letter, and then tuck in the shorter ends underneath to create a ball. Pinch the seam closed and drag the dough on the counter toward you once or twice to tighten the ball. You may see some of the green herbs begin to move their way towards the surface of the dough. If your dough is still very wet and sticking to the counter, you may find it helpful to use a bench scraper to assist in shaping your loaf.

Place the loaf with the seam facing up in the proofing basket. Cover the bread with a damp kitchen towel or plastic wrap and let it rise until doubled, 1 to 1½ hours. Meanwhile, preheat the oven to 425°F (218°C) and place a 7-quart (6.6-L) Dutch oven inside to preheat, as well, for at least 30 minutes.

Once the bread has risen, flip it out onto a piece of parchment paper. With a bread lame or a very sharp knife, slash into the top of the loaf an "X" shape or a different design of your choosing, such as leaves or circles. Be creative with it! Lift the parchment paper carefully into the Dutch oven. Sprinkle the top of the bread with the remaining asiago and cheddar cheese.

Close the Dutch oven and bake the bread, covered, for 40 minutes. Remove the lid and continue baking the loaf for 15 to 20 minutes, or until the bread is a deep golden brown and the cheese has become browned and crackly. The loaf should sound hollow when tapped upon with your fingertips or a spoon. Let the bread rest on the countertop for at least 1 hour before slicing.

Store the bread on the counter wrapped in plastic or a cloth bread bag for about 1 week.

¼ cup (10 g) chopped chives

¼ cup (15 g) chopped parsley

¾ cup (72 g) shredded asiago cheese, divided

½ cup (57 g) shredded mild cheddar cheese, divided

Rolled Brioche Bread

Soft and supple, true brioche bread is a dream come true. This bread is a labor of love, from start to finish, and the final result is something to be proud of. Brioche bread is similar in consistency to a bakery-style pastry like croissants, with heaps of butter and soft, pull-apart layers that will leave the dreamiest flavor in your mouth. Often brioche will be presented as a dinner roll or sandwich bun, but this bread is shaped like a milk bread, rolled up like a cinnamon roll, and baked in a loaf pan. It is both fun to look at and eat!

In a small saucepan over medium heat, warm the milk and sugar for 3 to 4 minutes, until it reaches 110°F (43°C). Remove the pan from the heat.

In the bowl of a standing electric mixer fitted with a paddle attachment, mix together 1 cup (125 g) of the flour and the yeast. Pour the warm milk mixture over the flour and yeast and turn the mixer to low-medium speed. Add in the salt and the eggs, one at a time, making sure each egg is well incorporated before adding in the next, about 5 minutes. Gradually add in the remaining 2¼ cups (281 g) of flour until the dough becomes a bit stiff and no longer clings to the sides of the bowl. Knead the dough like this for 15 to 20 minutes.

After the dough has been kneaded, begin to add in the butter. Add the pieces individually, waiting for the first piece to be incorporated into the dough before adding the next piece of butter. This should take about 10 minutes. Once all of the butter has been added to the bowl, knead the dough on medium speed for another 20 minutes. The longer the dough is kneaded, the better the structure of the gluten strands will be and the more tender your brioche will be as well.

Shape the final dough into a ball and place it into a large, lightly greased bowl. Cover the bowl with plastic wrap and let it rise on your countertop for about 1 hour. At this point, you can either shape the brioche and bake it, or you can let the dough develop a stronger flavor by having it go through a chilling period (see Tip). To chill the dough, place the bowl in the refrigerator and leave it for at least 8 to 12 hours or overnight.

Makes 1 loaf

6 tbsp (90 ml) whole milk

¼ cup (50 g) granulated sugar

3¼ cups (406 g) all-purpose flour, divided

2 tsp (8 g) active dry yeast

¼ tsp kosher salt

3 large eggs, room temperature

⅓ cup (77 g) salted butter, softened and sliced into ½-inch (1.3-cm) pieces

(continued)

The next morning, bring the dough out onto the counter and let it rest for about 30 minutes. Deflate the dough gently and divide it into three equal-sized pieces. If you did not chill your dough, you will begin your shaping process at this point.

Beginning with one piece of dough, roll it into a 4 x 10–inch (10 x 25–cm) rectangle. Fold the dough into thirds, like a business letter, overlapping the sides into a 2 x 10–inch (5 x 25–cm)-long rectangle. Starting from the shorter end, roll up the dough like a big cinnamon roll. Repeat with the remaining pieces of dough.

Place the rolled dough into a lightly greased 8½ x 4½ x 2¾–inch (22 x 11 x 7–cm) loaf pan, with the rolled sides facing the longest sides of the pan. Cover the pan with plastic wrap and let it rise until doubled or until an indentation made with your finger into the dough does not bounce back, 2½ to 3 hours, if the dough was chilled. If the dough was not chilled, this will take 45 minutes to 1 hour.

Meanwhile, preheat the oven to 375°F (191°C). Once the dough is ready to bake, whisk together the egg and water to make an egg wash. Brush this all over the top of the puffed dough. Bake the loaf for 40 to 50 minutes, covering the dough with foil for the last 20 minutes of baking to prevent over-browning. The bread is finished when it is a deep golden brown and the inner layers are no longer doughy. This can be checked by gently separating the layers with a paring knife.

Let the bread rest for about 10 minutes before serving it hot! To store the bread, leave it wrapped in foil at room temperature for about 5 days.

1 large egg + 1 tbsp (15 ml) water, for egg wash

Tip

Brioche requires lots of mixing time to develop the gluten strands that make it so incredibly soft and supple. The longer you can mix it, the better, and you will notice that the dough goes from sticky and buttery to smooth, soft, and elastic after at least 20 minutes of kneading. For a truly deep flavor, a chilling period must be done for this type of dough, which makes the entire process take longer than your average yeasted bread. If you do not mind having a less strong buttery flavor to this bread, then you do not have to chill it! It will still be incredibly soft and delicious.

Cinnamon Star Bread with Eggnog Icing

This beautiful Cinnamon Star Bread is the perfect addition to your holiday baking line up. With a soft, fluffy dough and a buttery, cinnamon-sugar filling, it brings about memories of romantic winter days sitting beside a glowing fire with snow gently falling outside cottage windows. This is a favorite cinnamon roll recipe transformed into something new, as you shape the dough carefully into a magical star or snowflake. The end result looks like a complicated pastry, but it is truly quite simple to make. Finish this sweet bread off with a drizzle of eggnog icing and a hot cup of chocolate!

To make the Cinnamon Star Bread, in a standing electric mixer fitted with a hook attachment, whisk together the warm water, yeast, and sugar. Leave the yeast to bloom for 5 to 7 minutes, or until it has grown and become bubbly.

Whisk in the salt, ½ cup (120 ml) of the melted butter, the eggs, and the vanilla. Begin mixing on low and slowly incorporating the flour, 1 cup (125 g) at a time, until a smooth and elastic dough forms. The dough is finished when it no longer clings to the sides of the bowl, 10 to 12 minutes. It should still be a bit wet and sticky, but it should not cling nor clump on your fingers. Shape the dough into a ball and place it into a lightly greased bowl. Cover the bowl with a damp kitchen towel or plastic wrap and let it rise until the dough has doubled, about 1 hour.

Gently deflate the dough with your hands, cover the bowl, and let it rest for another 15 minutes. Meanwhile, mix together the brown sugar and cinnamon in a small bowl. Line a large baking sheet with parchment paper.

With a sharp knife, divide the dough into four equal-sized pieces. On a lightly floured surface, roll out one piece of dough to a 10-inch (25-cm) circle. Transfer the dough to the prepared baking sheet.

Brush the circle of dough with about one-third of the remaining melted butter all the way to the edge. Sprinkle evenly with about one-third of the cinnamon and brown sugar mixture. Press the sugar mixture into the butter. Take another piece of the dough and roll it out to a 10-inch (25-cm) circle. Layer this on top of the dough that you just covered with butter and brown sugar mixture. Brush this next layer with one-third of the butter and sprinkle one-third of the brown sugar mixture over the top. Repeat this process with the third piece of dough, using up the remaining butter and brown sugar mixture. Roll out the remaining piece of dough and place it on top of the other layers.

(continued)

Makes 1 loaf

Cinnamon Star Bread

1 cup (240 ml) warm water

2 tbsp (24 g) active dry yeast

¼ cup (50 g) granulated sugar

1½ tsp kosher salt

1 cup (240 ml) melted salted butter, divided

2 large eggs

2 tsp (10 ml) vanilla extract

4½ cups (563 g) all-purpose flour

1 cup (194 g) brown sugar

1 tbsp (8 g) ground cinnamon

Place a drinking glass or a 3-inch (8-cm) biscuit cutter in the center of the circle of dough. This will be used as a guide to cut your star shape. Around the rim of the glass, make 16 small slits in the dough. With a serrated knife, slice through the layers to form 16 strips of dough; they should be a bit triangular in shape.

Using your hands, take two adjacent strips of dough and twist them away from each other, facing outwards, revealing the layers of cinnamon-sugar inside. Pinch the ends of both strips together to form a point. If they are not sticking well to each other, brush them with a bit of water. Repeat this process all of the way around the star until you have eight star points.

Cover the star with a damp kitchen towel or plastic wrap. Let it rise until slightly puffed, about 30 minutes. Meanwhile, preheat the oven to 375°F (191°C). In a small bowl, whisk together the egg and water to make the egg wash.

Brush the dough all over with the egg wash. Bake the star for 25 to 30 minutes, or until lightly golden brown and cooked through the middle. To check that the dough is fully baked, simply pull apart the inner layers a bit with a paring knife. Let the bread cool for about 20 minutes before icing.

To make the Eggnog Icing, in a medium bowl cream together the eggnog and butter. Whisk in the powdered sugar and vanilla until the icing has the consistency of molasses. Drizzle the star with icing and leave some extra for dunking!

To store the bread, leave it at room temperature wrapped in plastic for 4 to 5 days.

1 large egg + 1 tbsp (15 ml) water, for egg wash

Eggnog Icing

¼ cup (60 ml) eggnog

2 tbsp (28 g) salted butter, softened

2 cups (236 g) powdered sugar

1 tsp vanilla extract

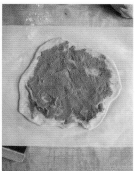

Everything Bagel Beer Pretzel Knots

After a long day of adventuring, you might imagine dropping into a fantastical tavern with stone walls and a roaring hearth. Settle in by the fire and enjoy the comforting taste of a soft pretzel, enriched with beer and served with a side of warm honey mustard cheese sauce. Flavored with Everything Bagel seasoning, these pretzels make an incredible appetizer or comfort food snack for your own cozy fantasy tavern.

To make the Everything Bagel Beer Pretzels, in the bowl of a standing electric mixer fitted with a dough hook, whisk together the warm water, beer, sugar, and yeast. Let the mixture stand for 8 to 10 minutes, until the yeast blooms, or has grown and becomes bubbly.

Whisk in the salt and butter. Slowly begin to incorporate the flour, 1 cup (125 g) at a time, until the dough begins to form and pull away from the sides of the bowl. Knead the dough for 6 to 8 minutes, or until it no longer clings to the sides of the bowl and is smooth, soft, and elastic. Place the dough into a large, lightly-greased bowl and cover it with plastic wrap or a damp kitchen towel. Let the dough rise until doubled, about 1 hour.

When the dough has doubled in size, gently deflate it with your hands. Transfer the dough to the countertop and divide it into 12 equal-sized pieces. Roll the pieces into 12-inch (30-cm) ropes. Loop the ropes into a single knot, tucking the ends underneath the knot and pinching them closed.

Line two baking sheets with parchment paper. Place the final shaped pretzels onto the baking sheets and cover them with plastic wrap or a damp kitchen towel. Let the pretzels rise until nearly doubled, 40 to 45 minutes.

(continued)

*Makes about
12 pretzel knots*

Everything Bagel Beer Pretzels

1 cup (240 ml) warm water

¾ cup (180 ml) light beer or apple cider, room temperature

½ cup (100 g) granulated sugar

2 tbsp (24 g) active dry yeast

2 tsp (12 g) kosher salt

1 tbsp (15 ml) melted salted butter

5 cups (625 g) all-purpose flour

While the pretzels rise, make the Honey Mustard Cheese Sauce. In a medium saucepan, melt the butter over medium-low heat. Whisk in the flour, making a roux, and cooking for 1 to 2 minutes, or until the flour gives off a nutty aroma. Slowly pour in the milk, whisking as you pour, bringing the sauce to a boil. It should thicken rather quickly. Then, add the cream, bringing it to a boil. Lower the heat to a simmer, then add the honey, mustard, and salt. Simmer the sauce for 2 to 4 minutes, or until it has thickened slightly. Remove the pot from the heat, then stir in the cheese until it has melted, 2 to 3 minutes.

Meanwhile, preheat the oven to 425°F (218°C). In a large pot, bring about 2 quarts (2 L) of water to a boil and stir in the baking soda until it is fully dissolved, about 2 minutes. Put two to three of the puffed pretzels into the boiling water, risen side down. Boil the pretzels for 1 minute and no longer. There is no need to flip the pretzels.

Remove the pretzels from the boiling water with a slotted spoon and transfer them back to the baking sheet, risen side facing up. Sprinkle the tops with the Everything Bagel seasoning. Let the water come back up a boil and repeat with the remaining pretzels and seasoning.

Once all of the pretzels have been boiled, bake them for 10 to 15 minutes in the preheated oven, or until they are a deep golden brown. Serve hot with the warm Honey Mustard Cheese Sauce.

To store the pretzels, keep them at room temperature wrapped in plastic or foil for about 1 week.

½ cup (110 g) baking soda

¼ cup (51 g) Everything Bagel seasoning

Honey Mustard Cheese Sauce

3 tbsp (44 g) salted butter

3 tbsp (24 g) all-purpose flour

1 cup (240 ml) whole milk

½ cup (120 ml) heavy cream

2 tbsp (30 ml) honey

2 tsp (10 ml) Dijon mustard

¼ tsp kosher salt

2 cups (226 g) cheddar cheese, shredded

Pain d'Epi

A French style bread, *pain d'epi*, or "cob bread" is a baguette that is cut and shaped like a wheat stalk. This charming loaf looks as if it should be growing in the countryside! This is an artisanal bread that is rather simple at its core, even though the shaping style makes it appear complicated. This is a charming stylistic change you can make to a yummy baguette with its crunchy crust and tender inner crumb. You can share this bucolic bread with others by pulling off each piece and spreading the little rolls with butter!

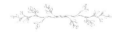

In a small saucepan, heat the water to 110°F (43°C).

In the bowl of a standing electric mixer fitted with a dough hook, pour the warm water into the bowl and sprinkle the yeast on top. Let the mixture sit, undisturbed, for about 10 minutes to allow the yeast to bloom, or grow and become bubbly. Whisk in the salt.

Gradually begin to add the flour, 1 cup (125 g) at a time, on low speed. Increase the speed as the dough begins to come together, kneading on medium-high speed for 6 to 8 minutes. It is ready when the dough no longer clings to the sides of the bowl and is smooth, elastic, and a little bit sticky. This dough in particular is very pillowy and soft.

Knead the dough on the countertop into a ball, pulling it toward you on the counter while simultaneously tucking the bottom of the dough underneath itself. Place the dough into a large, lightly-greased bowl and cover it with plastic wrap or a damp tea towel. Let the dough rest for about 15 minutes.

After the resting period, gently deflate the dough by pressing down on it. Stretch and pull the dough by lifting up a corner of it, pulling away from the dough, and folding it over the top of the dough ball. Repeat this all around the circle of dough and tuck the ends underneath, forming a new ball. Cover the bowl back up and let the dough rise until doubled, 1 to 1½ hours.

Deflate the dough again. Bring it onto your countertop and divide the dough into two equal-sized pieces. If necessary, lightly flour your countertop. Press the dough out on the counter with your fingertips into a 4 x 6–inch (10 x 15–cm) rectangle.

Makes 2 loaves

1½ cups (380 ml) water

2 tsp (8 g) active dry yeast

1½ tsp (9 g) kosher salt

4 cups (500 g) high-gluten bread flour or all-purpose flour, plus more for dusting

(continued)

To shape the baguette, fold half of the dough towards the center of the rectangle, like a business letter, and press it into the dough to seal. Fold the other half of the dough toward the center and press it in to seal.

Taking the edge of the dough, roll it over the center seam you just created and press the loaf together, pinching and rolling along the entire length of the little cylinder to enclose the loaf. Flip the loaf over with the seam on the counter, dragging the loaf toward you to close the seam and create some tension on the loaf. Once the bread is firmly sealed, roll it out into a log about 16 inches (40 cm) long. Taper the very ends of the bread to create pointy tips. Repeat with the second loaf of bread.

Transfer the shaped loaves to a couche or floured kitchen towel for the final proof. To create space for both loaves, pull up part of the fabric in between the two loaves; then cover the loaves with the remaining material or plastic wrap. Let the bread rise until nearly doubled, about 45 minutes. They are ready to bake when you make an indentation in the dough with your finger and it remains rather than popping back up.

While the loaves proof for a second time, preheat the oven to 475°F (246°C). Place a shallow pan of water in the bottom of the oven to create steam. Line an 18 x 13—inch (46 x 33—cm) baking sheet with parchment paper.

Once the loaves have puffed, it is time to shape them into wheat stalks. Carefully transfer the loaves to the prepared baking sheet. With a sharp pair of kitchen scissors, make a neat cut into the loaf crosswise, about 2 inches (5 cm) from the tapered end. Lift and set the piece of cut dough, which looks a bit like a leaf, to one side of the loaf. Make a second cut, another 2 inches (5 cm) above the previous cut, moving the dough over to the opposite side of the loaf. Repeat this process all up the length of the loaf, leaving the opposing tapered end straight. Shape the second loaf in a similar fashion.

Bake the loaves in the preheated oven for 20 to 25 minutes, or until the loaves are a deep golden brown and sound hollow when tapped upon with your fingertips or a spoon. Let the loaves rest for 15 to 20 minutes before pulling apart!

To store the bread, keep it at room temperature wrapped in plastic or a cloth bread bag for about 1 week.

Sweet Pineapple Clover Rolls

Your favorite brioche rolls are transformed into something positively sweet and fruity with a playful shape! Clovers, especially the rare four-leafed clover, have been mentioned in folklore for centuries. It was believed that children during the Middle Ages who carried four-leafed clovers would be able to catch sight of fairies! These rolls, shaped into clovers and baked in a muffin tin, are super soft and sweet. They are a perfect accompaniment to your rustic supper.

In a small saucepan over medium heat, warm the milk with the brown sugar. Stirring to dissolve the sugar, warm the milk to about 110°F (43°C), then remove the pan from the heat.

In the bowl of a standing electric mixer fitted with a dough hook, combine the warm milk and sugar with the yeast. Let the mixture sit for 8 to 10 minutes, or until the yeast has bloomed, or has grown and become bubbly. Stir in the salt, crushed pineapple, and the beaten eggs.

Slowly begin to incorporate the flour, 1 cup (125 g) at a time, until a soft dough begins to form. This dough may feel a little bit denser than other doughs in this book but continue to add as much flour as possible without drying out the dough completely. It should be smooth, elastic, and no longer clinging to the sides of the bowl while it is kneading, 15 to 20 minutes.

Once all or most of the flour has been added, begin to add in the butter, 1 tablespoon (14 g) at a time, waiting for the first piece to be well mixed in before adding the next. This should take about 10 minutes. Turn the mixer up to a medium speed and knead the butter into the dough for at least 20 minutes, or until the dough is soft, smooth, and elastic again. The texture will have changed from a dense dough to one that looks glossy and stretchy and perhaps a bit tacky.

With your hands, check if the gluten strands have strengthened enough by gently stretching a small part of the dough until it is super thin and see-through, like a windowpane. If this is possible, then the dough is ready. If not, then it should knead for another 5 to 10 minutes.

Shape the dough into a large ball and place it into a large, lightly-greased bowl. Cover the bowl with plastic wrap and let it rise for 1 hour, or until the dough has doubled.

Grease a standard 12-cup muffin tin and set this aside.

(continued)

Makes 12 rolls

¼ cup (60 ml) whole milk

¼ cup (49 g) light brown sugar, packed

2¼ tsp (9 g) active dry yeast

½ tsp kosher salt

20 oz (566 g) crushed pineapple

3 large eggs, lightly beaten

5 cups (625 g) bread flour

½ cup (116 g) salted butter, softened, plus more for serving

When the dough has doubled in size, gently deflate it with your hands. Turn the dough out onto the countertop and divide the dough into 12 equal-sized balls. To each small dough ball, divide it into three equal-sized balls. Stretch and shape the dough pieces into little, round balls, tucking the ends underneath like you would when shaping a bun.

Place the three small dough balls into one muffin cup, squishing them gently together. Repeat this with the rest of the dough, making 12 clover rolls. Cover the pan with plastic wrap and let the rolls rise until doubled, 45 to 60 minutes.

Meanwhile, preheat the oven to 350°F (177°C). In a small bowl, whisk together the egg and water to make an egg wash.

Once the rolls have doubled, brush the egg wash all over the tops of the rolls. Bake the rolls for 30 to 35 minutes, or until they are a deep golden brown on top and are baked through the middle without being doughy. To check this, gently pull apart the seam of one of the rolls with the tip of a paring knife. If the rolls are over-browning, cover them with a piece of tin foil for the last 10 minutes of baking. Serve the rolls warm with fresh butter!

Store the rolls at room temperature wrapped in plastic or foil for about 5 days.

1 large egg + 1 tbsp (15 ml) water, for egg wash

Cottage Sandwich Bread with Variations

The aroma of freshly baked bread invites a comforting and nostalgic feeling that evokes memories of slower, peaceful moments. There is no bread more ideal for cozy living than this soft, warm, and crusty cottage sandwich bread. A staple for everyday meals, this recipe, with its variations, is a testament to the joys of baking from scratch. Its texture is light and fluffy, and each version of this bread has a comforting flavor. It is the perfect companion to soups, sandwiches, and everything in between. Enjoy a slice with a warm pat of butter to remind yourself that often the best things in life are the simplest.

To make a White Cottage Bread loaf, in the bowl of a standing electric mixer fitted with a dough hook, whisk together the water, yeast, and sugar. Let the mixture rest for 5 to 6 minutes, until the yeast blooms, or grows and become bubbly. Stir in the salt and butter.

Slowly begin to incorporate the flour, 1 cup (125 g) at a time, until a soft dough forms. The dough is ready when it no longer clings to the sides of bowl, kneading on low speed for 8 to 10 minutes.

Knead the dough into a large ball and transfer it to a large, lightly greased bowl. Cover the bowl with plastic wrap or a damp kitchen towel and let it rise until doubled, about 1 hour.

After it has doubled in size, gently deflate the dough with your hands. Turn it out onto the countertop and shape it into a loaf. To do this, press the dough out into a rough 9 x 11–inch (22 x 28–cm) rectangle. Roll the loaf up from the shortest end like a jelly roll. Pinch the ends and the seam closed. Place the shaped loaf into a lightly greased 5 x 9–inch (13 x 22–cm) loaf pan. Cover the pan with plastic wrap or a damp kitchen towel and let it rise until nearly doubled, 45 to 50 minutes.

Preheat the oven to 375°F (191°C). Bake the loaf for about 40 minutes, or until it is a deep golden brown and the inside sounds hollow when tapped upon with your fingertips or a wooden spoon. Let the loaf rest in the pan for about 10 minutes before transferring it to a wire cooling rack to finish cooling. Let the loaf rest for at least 30 minutes before slicing.

(continued)

Makes 1 loaf

White Cottage Bread

1½ cups (360 ml) warm water

1 tbsp (12 g) active dry yeast

1 tbsp (15 g) granulated sugar

1½ tsp (9 g) kosher salt

1 tbsp (14 g) salted butter, softened

4 cups (500 g) all-purpose flour

To make a Honey Wheat Cottage Bread loaf, follow the instructions for the White Cottage Bread, but substitute in the honey for the granulated sugar. Add in the whole wheat flour first, then add in as much of the all-purpose flour as you can without drying out the dough. Follow the rest of the directions as stated on the previous page.

To make an Ancient Grain and Seed Cottage Bread loaf, follow the instructions for the White Cottage Bread, but substitute in the brown sugar for the granulated sugar. Combine the pumpkin seeds, sunflower kernels, poppy seeds, sesame seeds, and flax seeds in a small bowl. Reserve about 2 tablespoons (10 g) of the seeds. Place the rest in the bowl with the water, yeast, and brown sugar to soak for about 10 minutes. Add the salt and butter, as previously instructed. Finally, incorporate the spelt flour first, followed by as much all-purpose flour as the dough can handle without drying it out. Follow the rest of the directions as stated on the previous page. After shaping the loaf into a sandwich shape, roll the loaf in the reserved 2 tablespoons (10 g) of seeds. Then let the bread rise and bake as previously directed.

Store the bread at room temperature wrapped in plastic or foil for about 1 week.

Honey Wheat Cottage Bread

1½ cups (380 ml) warm water

1 tbsp (12 g) active dry yeast

1 tbsp (15 g) honey

1½ tsp (9 g) kosher salt

1 tbsp (14 g) salted butter, softened

1½ cups (180 g) whole wheat flour

2½ cups (313 g) all-purpose flour

Ancient Grain and Seed Cottage Bread

1½ cups (380 ml) warm water

1 tbsp (12 g) active dry yeast

1 tbsp (15 g) light brown sugar

3 tbsp (27 g) pumpkin seeds

3 tbsp (24 g) sunflower kernels

2 tbsp (18 g) poppy seeds

2 tbsp (18 g) sesame seeds

2 tbsp (20 g) flax seeds

1½ tsp (9 g) kosher salt

1 tbsp (14 g) salted butter, softened

1 cup (120 g) spelt flour

3 cups (375 g) all-purpose flour

Romantic Café Pastries

This chapter is inspired by the cafés and pâtisseries of childhood dreams. Romantic and fancy, these little desserts are decorated to the nines with bright pastel colors, fresh fruit, and edible flowers. I wanted each of these desserts to be just as dreamy to look at as they were to eat and to showcase what I had always romanticized about the cottage lifestyle when I was child.

You will fall in love with the tender and flaky Classic Croissants Dipped in Chocolate (page 119) and Lemon Cream Cheese Danishes (page 128). If you want something more decadent, try the Dulce de Leche Cream Horns (page 139) or Chocolate Hazelnut Choux au Craquelin (page 125). To satisfy your savory side, enjoy the Puff Pastry Croque Madame (page 133), or Tomato and Gruyère Puff Pastry Tarts (page 134).

Everything about this collection of pastries makes you feel as if you were transported to a sweet, little corner of a charming European city with cobblestone streets where they serve tiny cups of espresso and sell fresh flowers outside. I hope that you feel the charm of these pastries at home in your kitchen.

Classic Croissants Dipped in Chocolate

The charm of these chocolate-dipped croissants is only made more whimsical with the addition of dried rose petals and chopped nuts. These look and taste as if they came from your favorite pâtisserie. Layers and layers of dough all rolled together become the most incredible flaky pastry. It can be intimidating to try making croissants at home, but after lots and lots of experimentation, I have found that this recipe turns out beautifully every time. Then the fun part comes—decorating the croissants! My favorite part is slicing into them to see the many layers.

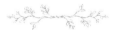

In the bowl of a standing electric mixer fitted with a paddle attachment, beat the butter with ⅓ cup (42 g) of the flour until it has become smooth and pasty, 3 to 5 minutes. The butter should be malleable enough to roll out and remain solid, like play dough.

Place it on a piece of wax paper. Place another piece of wax paper on top of the butter and press it down to flatten it with your hand or a rolling pin. If possible, avoid touching the butter much at all with your hands. Roll the butter into a 12-inch (30-cm) square in between the two sheets of wax paper. Place the butter block onto a baking sheet and pop it into the refrigerator for about 1 hour or the freezer for 30 minutes.

Meanwhile, begin making the croissant dough. In the same bowl from the standing mixer, now fitted with a dough hook, whisk together 2 cups (250 g) of the flour, the yeast, and the salt. There is no need to clean the bowl in between making the butter block and the dough.

In a small saucepan over medium heat, warm the milk and sugar together, whisking until the sugar dissolves and the milk is warm to the touch, about 110°F (44°C), 2 to 3 minutes. Add the milk mixture to the flour, yeast, and salt. Stir on low speed for about 1 minute. Beat on medium to high speed until the flour becomes completely absorbed, 2 to 3 minutes. Begin to incorporate the remaining flour, as much as possible, until the dough no longer clings to the sides of the bowl, 5 to 7 minutes. The dough should be a bit wet and elastic, but it should not stick nor cling to your hands. Cover the bowl with plastic wrap or a damp kitchen towel and let it rest for about 15 minutes.

On a lightly floured surface, roll out the dough to a 14-inch (35-cm) square, being careful to roll all the way to the edge of the dough so that it is as even as possible. Brush off any excess flour with a pastry brush.

(continued)

Makes 16 pastries

Classic Croissants (see Tip [page 121])

1½ cups (341 g) salted butter, slightly softened

4½ cups (564 g) all-purpose flour, divided, plus more for dusting

1 tbsp (12 g) active dry yeast

¼ tsp kosher salt

1¼ cups (300 ml) whole milk

¼ cup (50 g) granulated sugar

Remove the butter block from the fridge or freezer. Remove one piece of the wax paper. Invert the butter block onto the dough, turning it so that it sits at a 45-degree angle, like a diamond inside of a square. With your hands, pull the corners of the dough into the center of the butter block and pinch the seams closed. The butter should be completely enclosed in the dough. Dust the top of the dough with a bit of flour and flip it over on the countertop.

With a rolling pin, gently smack the dough to begin flattening it. Roll the dough into a 20 x 12–inch (50 x 30–cm) rectangle. Brush off any excess flour. Fold the dough into thirds, like a business letter. It is important to make sure that the edges line up squarely and that no butter has escaped through the edges of the dough; if necessary, trim the edges to square them off. Loosely wrap the dough in plastic wrap, place it on a baking sheet, and chill it in the refrigerator for 1 hour or the freezer for 30 minutes.

After the croissant dough has chilled, roll it back out to a 20 x 12–inch (50 x 30–cm) rectangle, first rolling in the direction of the shortest ends. Fold the dough into thirds again, wrap, and then chill in the refrigerator for 1 hour or the freezer for 30 minutes. Repeat this process two more times, for a total of four laminations, or foldings. On the final lamination, wrap the dough in plastic wrap and chill in the refrigerator for 8 to 12 hours or overnight.

In the morning, the dough will have puffed in its wrapping. Remove it from the refrigerator. On a lightly floured surface, roll it out to a 16 x 12–inch (40 x 30–cm) rectangle. With a sharp knife, trim off any ends that are rounded so the dough is completely squared off. With a tape measure, go along the top longest edge of the dough and make a small cut with the knife every 4 inches (10 cm). On the bottom longest edge, make a cut at 2 inches (5 cm) and then continue from that point with a cut every 4 inches (10 cm). These cuts will help you to divide the croissants into perfect triangles.

From the top edge, at the first 4-inch (10-cm) cut, slice diagonally down the dough to meet at the bottom 2-inch (5-cm) cut. Continue this process with the remaining dough, creating 16 pieces of triangular dough.

Once the croissants are cut, make a small cut at the bottom edge of each triangle, about 1 inch (2.5 cm) long. The ending result will look like an Eiffel Tower. With your hands, gently stretch the triangle to about twice its length, being careful not to break the dough. With the edge you just sliced, roll up the croissant, with the little tower legs spreading out as you roll. Roll it up tightly. If the dough is heavily floured, brush most of the flour away first before rolling. Repeat with the remaining croissants.

Place the finished croissants on two greased baking sheets. Cover the croissants with plastic wrap and place into the refrigerator for about 30 minutes. Once chilled again, let them rise on the counter or in a warm spot until puffed and jiggly when shaken, about 1 hour. They are ready to bake when an indentation from your finger remains in the dough.

In a small dish, whisk together the egg and 1 tablespoon (15 ml) of water. Brush the croissants with the egg wash. Bake the croissants in a 425°F (218°C) oven for 15 minutes. Reduce the oven temperature to 375°F (191°C) and bake for another 10 to 15 minutes, or until the croissants are a deep golden brown and are no longer doughy at the inner layers of lamination. Let the croissants cool for about 30 minutes on wire cooling racks.

To decorate the croissants, melt the white chocolate and semisweet chocolate in separate microwave-safe bowls. Dip the cooled croissants into the melted chocolate or drizzle with the melted chocolate. Place the dipped croissants on pieces of parchment paper on the countertop to harden. While the chocolate is still wet, sprinkle the tops of the croissants with rose petals and chopped nuts of your choice.

Croissants will keep on the counter for about 5 days stored in an airtight container or can be frozen for about 2 months.

1 large egg + 1 tbsp (15 ml) water, for egg wash

Chocolate Decorations

½ cup (85 g) white baking chocolate chips

½ cup (85 g) semisweet baking chocolate chips

¼ cup (10 g) dried rose petals

½ cup (49 g) chopped assorted nuts, such as walnuts, pecans, and pistachios

Tip

To make croissants that have perfect, flaky layers, you'll want to make sure that the space you are making them in is chilly. This is not always possible depending on where you live or the season you are in. Our homes are not built like a professional bakery! To help balance out the temperature, it is a good idea to use ice packs on the countertop in between laminations of the dough. Make sure you leave enough room in your fridge or freezer to chill the dough in between rolling!

Strawberry Cheesecake Cruffins

There is something undeniably charming about the artisanal and rustic look of cruffins. A truly whimsical combination of the classic croissant and humble muffin, the cruffin is a playful and inventive twist on a traditional pastry. You may prefer to enjoy your cruffin left plain, but they taste even more dreamy filled with this strawberry cheesecake cream filling. Sweet and tangy, it's a lovely tribute to the season, evoking images of sun-filled strawberry patches.

Make the croissant dough according to the directions on page 119, up to the stage of chilling the final dough for 8 to 12 hours or overnight.

Grease a jumbo muffin tin with cooking spray and set this aside.

Once your croissant dough has chilled, roll it out to a 14 x 20–inch (35 x 50–cm) rectangle, trimming any rounded edges so that they are perfectly squared. Cut the rectangle into 1½ x 14–inch (4 x 35–cm) strips. Cut the strips in half crosswise so that they are about 7 inches (18 cm) long. Stretch each strip with your hands until they are about 8 inches (20 cm) long.

Layer three strips over each other, stacking them so that they are about 1 inch (2.5 cm) offset from each other. Starting from the short end where the layers are offset from each other, begin to roll up the cruffin like a jellyroll. Roll the strips as tightly as possible. You should end up with a spiral that looks like a cinnamon roll with three tails off the side.

Tuck the tails underneath the bottom of the cruffin, pinching the edge of the tail with the bottom edge of the cruffin and enclosing the bottom of the roll. Place the spiral side up in the muffin tin. Repeat with the remaining strips until you have six cruffins.

Cover the cruffins with plastic wrap or a damp tea towel. Let the cruffins rise until doubled in size, the layers are visible, and they jiggle slightly when lightly shaken. This will take 1½ to 2 hours, depending on the temperature of your kitchen (see Tip [page 124]).

Preheat the oven to 425°F (218°C).

(continued)

Makes about 6 cruffins

1 recipe Classic Croissants (page 119)

In a small bowl, whisk together the egg and water. Brush this all over the cruffins and sprinkle the coarse sugar over the tops. With your finger or a chopstick, make a hole in the center of the layers of the cruffins to create space for the filling.

Bake the cruffins for 20 minutes. Reduce the oven temperature to 375°F (191°C) and bake for another 10 to 15 minutes, or until the cruffins are a deep golden brown and the layers are no longer doughy. You may check this by gently pulling apart the layers with a paring knife. Allow the cruffins to cool completely before filling.

To make the Strawberry Cheesecake Filling, whip the heavy cream with the powdered sugar in a medium bowl until it reaches stiff peaks, or the tips stand straight, 5 to 6 minutes. Set this aside.

Cream together the cream cheese, strawberry jam, freeze-dried strawberries, and vanilla. Fold in half of the whipped cream until incorporated, 1 to 2 minutes, then fold in the second half. The resulting cream will be a beautiful light pink color and have a fluffy texture. Transfer the cheesecake filling to a piping bag fitted with a large round tip or cut off the end of the bag with scissors.

Pipe the cheesecake filling into the center of the cruffins. If the center openings closed while baking, use the end of a wooden spoon or chopstick to create a new opening by separating the layers. Let some of the filling pop out of the cruffin, and stick either a whole or halved strawberry on top. Dust the cruffins with powdered sugar. Serve the cruffins at room temperature.

Store the cruffins in the refrigerator for 3 to 4 days.

1 egg + 1 tbsp (15 ml) water, for egg wash

1 tbsp (15 g) coarse sugar

Strawberry Cheesecake Filling

1 cup (240 ml) heavy cream

½ cup (59 g) powdered sugar

4 oz (113 g) cream cheese, softened

¼ cup (60 ml) strawberry jam

2 tbsp (2 g) finely ground freeze-dried strawberries

½ tsp vanilla extract

3 to 6 whole strawberries, for decorating

Powdered sugar, for dusting

Tip

To speed up the proofing time for your cruffins, place a pan of boiling hot water in the bottom of your oven. Place the covered cruffins in the center rack of your oven and close the door. This creates a perfectly humid and warm environment for the cruffins to rise!

Chocolate Hazelnut Choux au Craquelin

There is nothing so enchanting as a beautifully decorated cream puff! Each deliciously rich chocolate puff is filled with a white chocolate hazelnut ganache and crowned with a crisp, crackly cookie topping that shimmers like stardust. These exquisite pastries are wonderful to serve at any occasion, but they look especially beautiful at a fancy dinner! Before serving, decorate each adorable pastry with intricate designs made from chocolate and chopped hazelnuts to create a truly divine dessert.

Begin by making the Chocolate Hazelnut Craquelin. In a standing electric mixer fitted with a paddle attachment, cream together the butter and brown sugar until it is light and fluffy, 3 to 4 minutes. Mix in the flour, cocoa powder, and hazelnut extract. The mixture will be dry at first, but it will eventually form into a solid ball after 4 to 5 minutes of beating on medium-high speed.

Transfer the craquelin to a piece of parchment or wax paper. Place a second piece of parchment or wax paper over the ball of craquelin and press it flat with your hands. With a rolling pin, roll out the craquelin to about ¼ inch (6 mm) thick. Place the craquelin in between the sheets of parchment on a baking sheet and freeze for about 30 minutes.

After the craquelin is chilled, cut it with a 3-inch (8-cm) biscuit cutter. Cut out 12 pieces. If you need to, ball the craquelin back up and roll out again to create more pieces. If you have craquelin leftover, simply wrap it in plastic wrap and freeze it for a later date. Lay out the cut craquelin pieces for this recipe on a baking sheet and freeze until ready to use.

Next, make the Hazelnut Ganache. Bring a small saucepan of water to a simmer. Place a medium heat-safe bowl over the simmering water. Add the heavy cream, white chocolate chips, and hazelnut paste to the bowl. Stir continually until all of the chocolate has melted and the mixture is well combined, 10 to 12 minutes. Remove the bowl from the heat and cover it with plastic wrap.

Place the bowl in the refrigerator and stir the ganache every 10 minutes to help it cool down faster. Once the ganache is thick, remove it from the fridge and whip it with a heavy wire whisk. This will happen quickly, 4 to 5 minutes. Transfer the whipped ganache to a piping bag fitted with a star tip and refrigerate until ready to use.

(continued)

Makes about
12 cream puffs

Chocolate Hazelnut Craquelin

½ cup (116 g) butter, softened

½ cup (97 g) light brown sugar, packed

¾ cup (94 g) all-purpose flour

2 tbsp (12 g) Dutch cocoa powder

1 tsp hazelnut extract

Hazelnut Ganache

2 cups (480 ml) heavy cream

3 cups (450 g) white chocolate chips

4 oz (113 g) hazelnut paste

After the craquelin and ganache are made, make the Chocolate Choux Pastry. Preheat the oven to 400°F (204°C) and line a large baking sheet with a silicone mesh mat or parchment paper.

In a medium saucepan, melt the butter in the water over medium heat. Once the butter has fully melted, 2 to 3 minutes, stir in the salt, flour, cocoa powder, and sugar. It will create a thick paste. Remove the pan from the heat as soon as the paste is formed and place it on the countertop. Let the mixture rest for about 10 minutes before the next step.

With a wooden spoon, stir in the eggs one at a time, fully mixing in each egg before adding the next. With each egg addition, the mixture will become gloppy and separated, but it will soon turn into a satiny and glossy batter after a few minutes.

Transfer the choux dough to a piping bag fitted with a ½-inch (1.3-cm)-diameter round piping tip. Pipe the choux dough onto the prepared baking sheet, making each cream puff about 2 x 2–inches (5 x 5–cm) across and 3 inches (8 cm) apart. There should be enough dough for about 12 cream puffs.

Place a piece of chilled craquelin on top of each cream puff. Do not press the cream puffs flat, just rest it on top of the pastry dough.

Bake the cream puffs in the preheated oven for 40 to 45 minutes. During the last 10 minutes of baking, poke two small holes into the sides of the cream puff with a toothpick to let air escape and help dry out the inside. The inside of the cream puff should be dry and not soggy, and the outside should be a dark chocolate brown. Place the finished cream puffs on a wire cooling rack to cool to room temperature before assembling.

To assemble the cream puffs, slice off the top half of the pastry with a serrated knife. Divide the chocolate hazelnut spread evenly amongst the bottoms of each cream puff. With the Hazelnut Ganache, pipe it over the chocolate hazelnut spread and out of the top of the cream puff, making a swirled design. Place the top of the cream puff over the piped ganache. Finish with a drizzle of melted chocolate and chopped hazelnuts decorated on the tops and sides of the cream puff. Serve the cream puffs chilled.

To store the cream puffs, keep them in the refrigerator for 3 to 4 days.

Chocolate Choux Pastry

½ cup (116 g) salted butter

1 cup (240 ml) water

½ tsp kosher salt

1 cup (120 g) cake flour

1 tbsp (6 g) Dutch cocoa powder

2 tbsp (30 g) granulated sugar

3 large eggs

1 cup (280 g) chocolate hazelnut spread

Melted chocolate, for drizzling

Chopped hazelnuts, for decorating

Lemon Cream Cheese Danishes

Made similarly to croissant dough, the dough for Danishes has a slight difference in that it includes eggs to create a truly delicious rich, sweet, and flaky dough. This Danish pastry includes cardamom to elevate the incredible flavor. The best part about making these pretty breakfast pastries is the different shaping options! Learn to make the Danish pocket, pinwheel, and envelope to house the rich and creamy Lemon Cream Cheese Filling. You may choose whichever shape you like!

In the bowl of a standing electric mixer fitted with a paddle attachment, beat the butter with ⅓ cup (42 g) of the bread flour until it has become smooth and pasty, 3 to 5 minutes. The butter should be malleable enough to roll out and remain solid, like play dough.

Place it on a piece of wax paper. Place another piece of wax paper on top of the butter and press it down to flatten it with your hand or a rolling pin. If possible, avoid touching the butter much at all with your hands. Roll the butter into a 12-inch (30-cm) square in between the two sheets of wax paper. Place the butter block onto a baking sheet and pop it into the refrigerator for about 1 hour or the freezer for 30 minutes.

Meanwhile, begin making the Danish Pastry dough. In the same bowl from the standing mixer, now fitted with a dough hook, whisk together 2 cups (250 g) of the bread flour, the yeast, the cardamom, and the salt. There is no need to clean the bowl in between making the butter block and making the dough.

In a small saucepan over medium heat, warm the milk and sugar together, whisking until the sugar dissolves and the milk is warm to the touch, about 110°F (44°C), or 2 to 3 minutes. Add the milk mixture to the flour, yeast, and salt. Stir on low speed for about 1 minute. Add the egg and egg yolks. Beat on medium to high speed until the flour becomes completely absorbed, 2 to 3 minutes.

Begin to incorporate the remaining bread flour along with the cake flour, as much as possible, until the dough no longer clings to the sides of the bowl, 5 to 7 minutes. The dough should be a bit wet and elastic, but it should not stick nor cling to your hands. Cover the bowl with plastic wrap or a damp kitchen towel and let it rest for about 15 minutes.

On a lightly floured surface, roll out the dough to a 14-inch (35-cm) square, being careful to roll all the way to the edge of the dough so that it is as even as possible. Brush off any excess flour with a pastry brush.

(continued)

Makes about 12 pastries

Danish Pastry

1½ cups (348 g) salted butter, slightly softened

3½ cups (437 g) high-gluten bread flour, divided

1 tbsp (12 g) active dry yeast

½ tsp cardamom

¼ tsp kosher salt

1¼ cups (300 ml) whole milk

¼ cup (50 g) granulated sugar

1 large egg

2 egg yolks

1 cup (120 g) cake flour

Remove the butter block from the fridge or freezer. Remove one piece of the wax paper. Invert the butter block onto the dough, turning it so that it sits at a 45-degree angle, like a diamond inside of a square. With your hands, pull the corners of the dough into the center of the butter block and pinch the seams closed. The butter should be completely enclosed in the dough. Dust the top of the dough with a bit of flour and flip it over on the countertop.

With a rolling pin, gently smack the dough to begin flattening it. Roll the dough into 20 x 12–inch (50 x 30–cm) rectangle. Brush off any excess flour. Fold the dough into thirds, like a business letter. It is important to make sure that the edges line up squarely and that no butter has escaped through the edges of the dough; if necessary, trim the edges to square them off. Loosely wrap the dough in plastic wrap, place on a baking sheet, and chill it in the refrigerator for 1 hour or the freezer for 30 minutes.

After the Danish dough has chilled, roll it back out to a 20 x 12–inch (50 x 30–cm) rectangle, first rolling in the direction of the shortest ends. Fold the dough into thirds again, wrap, and then chill. Repeat this process two more times, for a total of four laminations, or foldings. On the final lamination, wrap the dough in plastic wrap and chill in the refrigerator for 8 to 12 hours or overnight.

In the morning, the dough will have puffed in its wrapping. Remove it from the refrigerator. On a lightly floured surface, roll it out to a 12-inch (30-cm) square. With a sharp knife, trim off any ends that are rounded so the dough is completely squared off. Cut the dough into 3-inch (8-cm) squares, leaving you with 12 pieces. Place the pieces on a large baking sheet lined with parchment paper to chill while you make the filling.

To make the Lemon Cream Cheese Filling, in a small bowl, beat together the cream cheese and powdered sugar. Set this aside along with the lemon curd.

Preheat the oven to 425°F (218°C). In a small bowl, whisk together the egg and water to make an egg wash.

Lemon Cream Cheese Filling

8 oz (226 g) cream cheese, softened

¼ cup (30 g) powdered sugar

¾ cup (180 ml) lemon curd

1 egg + 1 tbsp (15 ml) water, for egg wash

Coarse sugar, for dusting

Fresh lemon slices, for decorating

Next, shape the Danish pastries. You may choose several designs. I love the look of a windowpane Danish! Once the Danishes are shaped, brush them all over with the egg wash. Fill the centers of each Danish with about 1 tablespoon (15 ml) of the Lemon Cream Cheese Filling. Place a 1-tablespoon (15-ml) dollop of lemon curd on top the cream cheese. Sprinkle the Danishes with the coarse sugar.

Bake the Danishes for about 10 minutes. Then lower the oven temperature to 375°F (191°C). Continue to bake the Danishes for another 15 to 20 minutes, or until they are a deep golden brown and the inner layers are baked through and no longer doughy. To check, gently pull apart the layers with a paring knife.

Serve the Danishes warm or at room temperature with fresh lemon slices for decoration. To store the Danishes, keep them in the refrigerator wrapped in plastic or an airtight container for about 5 days.

To make pinwheels: Cut each corner of the square of pastry three-quarters of the way toward the center. Fold every other point toward the center. Press the center together to seal. For a better seal, brush the corners and the center with the egg wash.

To make a Danish pocket: Cut each corner of the square of pastry three-quarters of the way toward the center. Take each corner and pull it toward the center of the square. Press the center together to seal. For a better seal, brush the corners and center with egg wash. Add the filling in the center where the points meet.

To make an envelope: Fold the square of pastry in half diagonally. Make two diagonal cuts along the outside edge, leaving about ¼ inch (6 mm) of the outside edge, so that it looks like a border. Unfold the dough. Take the outer edge, or the "frame," and fold it over until it meets the inner edge. Fold the other outer edge in a similar fashion. This will create a diamond shape. For a better seal, brush the edges with egg wash and pinch together.

Puff Pastry Croque Madame

I cannot think of a more delicious breakfast than Croque Madame. The origins of the Croque Madame are born from the Croque Monsieur, a sandwich fried in cheese and adorned with a creamy Mornay sauce. This sandwich hails from France. However, it is the addition of a fried egg that makes it a "madame." This particular recipe transforms the classic sandwich into something fresh! Easily bake up a batch of pastries that fit easily into your hands, delicately folded in flaky, buttery layers of puff pastry. The flavors truly come alive with each bite of a pastry, runny egg yolk, and a rich, cheesy Mornay sauce.

Preheat the oven to 425°F (218°C) and line a baking sheet with parchment paper.

In a small saucepan, melt the butter over medium heat and then whisk in the flour. Cook the roux until it turns a light brown and gives off a nutty aroma, 1 to 2 minutes. Slowly pour in the milk, whisking as you do so, bringing it to a boil. It should thicken up rather quickly. Pour in the cream in a similar manner, lowering the heat to a simmer once it has begun to boil and has thickened. Add the onion powder, salt, pepper, and cloves and simmer the sauce for about 5 minutes.

Remove the pan from the heat and stir in the Gruyère, Parmesan, and Dijon mustard. Cover the pot with a lid and set it aside while you prepare the pastries.

Cut the puff pastry into eight 3-inch (8-cm) squares. Arrange the pastry squares about 2 inches (5 cm) apart on the prepared baking sheet. In a small bowl, whisk together the egg and water to make an egg wash.

For each pastry, brush with the egg wash all over. Pour about 2 tablespoons (30 ml) of Mornay Sauce over the tops of the pastries. Then, layer on a piece of ham and a sprinkle of Gruyère cheese. Bake the pastries in the preheated oven for 10 to 15 minutes.

Remove the pastries from the oven. With a spoon, make a small impression in the center of the pastries and crack open an egg into each indent. Place the pastries back into the oven and bake for another 10 to 15 minutes, or until the whites of the eggs are set and the yolk is still runny.

Serve the pastries hot with fresh chives, flaky sea salt, and freshly cracked pepper. Use any leftover Mornay Sauce for serving. Store the pastries in the refrigerator wrapped in plastic for about 3 days.

Makes 8 pastries

Mornay Sauce

2 tbsp (29 g) salted butter

2 tbsp (16 g) all-purpose flour

1 cup (240 ml) whole milk

½ cup (120 ml) heavy cream

1 tsp onion powder

1 tsp kosher salt

½ tsp freshly cracked black pepper

¼ tsp ground cloves

½ cup (59 g) Gruyère cheese, shredded

¼ cup (30 g) Parmesan cheese, grated

1 tbsp (15 ml) Dijon mustard

Croque Madame Pastries

1 sheet (260 g) frozen puff pastry, thawed

1 large egg + 1 tbsp (15 ml) water, for egg wash

9 oz (255 g) black forest ham

1 cup (118 g) Gruyère cheese, shredded

8 large eggs

¼ cup (10 g) fresh chives, chopped, for serving

Flaky sea salt, for serving

Freshly cracked black pepper, for serving

Tomato and Gruyère Puff Pastry Tarts

Be careful not to overlook this seemingly simple recipe! It is a delicious nod to summer gatherings held under a tangling of leafy branches and the feeling of a gentle breeze sending over the scent of the earthy tomato vines. As you plan your lunch spread, these tiny tarts topped with garden fresh tomatoes make an ideal appetizer to serve. The acidity from the tomato paired with buttery puff pastry, gooey Gruyère cheese, and flaky sea salt will leave you coming back to fill your plate!

Prepare two wire cooling racks and layer them with paper towels. Begin by slicing the tomatoes into ¼-inch (6-mm) slices. Lay the sliced tomatoes across the paper towels without overlapping them and sprinkle them with 1 tablespoon (18 g) of the salt. Let them sweat for about 30 minutes. After they have released most of their juices, blot them with more paper towels to help dry them.

Preheat the oven to 425°F (218°C). Line two large baking sheets with parchment paper and set them aside.

With a 2-inch (5-cm) round biscuit cutter, begin cutting out pieces of the puff pastry. There should be about 24 pieces. Arrange the cut pastry on the baking sheets, about 2 inches (5 cm) apart.

In a small bowl, whisk together the egg and water to make the egg wash. Brush the pastries all over with the egg wash.

Sprinkle the Gruyère cheese over all of the pastries evenly, then top each pastry with a slice of tomato. Season the pastries with the remaining 1 tablespoon (18 g) of salt and the pepper.

Bake the tarts for 20 to 25 minutes, or until the pastry is golden brown and puffed, and the cheese is melted and bubbly. Serve the tarts hot or at room temperature. These store beautifully in the fridge in an airtight container for about 5 days, and they can be reheated to enjoy at a later date.

Makes about 24 tarts

4 medium Roma tomatoes (240 g)

2 tbsp (36 g) flaky sea salt, divided

1 sheet (260 g) frozen puff pastry, thawed

1 large egg + 1 tbsp (15 ml) water, for egg wash

1 cup (118 g) Gruyère cheese, shredded

1 tsp freshly cracked pepper

Raspberry Pistachio Éclairs

Let's wander into a whimsical culinary journey with the inspiration of charming and quaint pâtisseries brimming with charmingly decorated desserts that tickle the imagination. These delectable treats are a feast for the senses with a perfect balance of sweetness and rich, nutty pistachios. With each bite of light and airy classic choux pastry, you will find a creamy pistachio center and delightfully tart raspberry glaze. They are so pretty, topped with fresh raspberries and little dots of pistachio pastry cream and chopped pistachios. These will most certainly satisfy your sweet tooth!

Begin by making the Pistachio Pastry Cream. In a medium saucepan, cover the pistachios completely with water. Bring the water to a boil and boil the pistachios on medium-high heat for 5 to 6 minutes. Remove the pan from the heat and drain the pistachios.

Once cool enough to handle, spread the pistachios on one half of a clean tea towel and cover the pistachios with the other half. With your hands, roll them around to remove the skins. Picking out the nuts and discarding the skins, blend the pistachios and ¼ cup (60 ml) of the milk in a food processor or with a mortar and pestle until a paste forms. Set aside for later use.

In a medium bowl, whisk together the egg yolks and sugar. Whisk for about 4 minutes, or until the yolks have turned pale yellow and the mixture is thick and syrupy. Whisk in the cake flour, cornstarch, and the pistachio paste until the mixture is no longer dry, 1 to 2 minutes.

To the same medium saucepan that was used for boiling the pistachios, add the remaining 1¾ cups (420 ml) of milk. Warm the milk over medium heat until it just begins to simmer around the edges of the pan but is not boiling. Pour about 2 tablespoons (30 ml) of the milk into the pistachio and egg mixture to temper the eggs, whisking until it is well incorporated. Then, slowly add the pistachio mixture into the pan of hot milk, whisking constantly to prevent any sticking.

Whisking the custard constantly, cook it over low heat until it thickens to a consistency that is thick, stiff, and smooth, similar to commercial mayonnaise. Continue to whisk for another 1 to 2 minutes, after the custard has reached its peak thickness, and it will begin to become glossy and thin out slightly.

Makes about 14 éclairs

Pistachio Pastry Cream

½ cup (76 g) hulled pistachios

2 cups (480 ml) whole milk, divided

4 large egg yolks

⅓ cup (67 g) granulated sugar

2 tbsp (16 g) cake flour

2 tbsp (16 g) cornstarch

2 tbsp (29 g) salted butter, cubed

2 tsp (10 ml) almond extract

Green food coloring, optional

Remove the custard from the heat. With an immersion blender, or a food processor, pulse the finished custard, butter, and almond extract until the butter has been fully incorporated and the custard is thin and smooth. Cover the custard with plastic wrap that is touching the surface of it and place it in the refrigerator until it is fully chilled, about 3 hours. To speed up the process, place the custard in a flatter dish like a pie pan or cake pan.

Preheat the oven to 400°F (204°C). Line two baking sheets with a silicone mesh baking mat or parchment paper and set them aside.

While the pastry cream is chilling, make the Choux Pastry. In a medium saucepan, melt the butter in the water over medium heat. Once the butter has fully melted, 2 to 3 minutes, stir in the salt, cake flour, and sugar. Continue to stir until it becomes a thick, creamy paste, about 4 minutes. Remove the pan from the heat as soon as the paste is formed and place it on the countertop. Let the mixture rest for about 10 minutes before the next step.

Choux Pastry

1 cup (232 g) salted butter

2 cups (480 ml) water

1 tsp kosher salt

2 cups (240 g) cake flour

¼ cup (50 g) granulated sugar

6 large eggs

¼ cup (30 g) powdered sugar

(continued)

With a wooden spoon, stir in the eggs one at a time, fully mixing in each egg before adding the next. With each egg addition, the mixture will become gloppy and separated, but it will soon turn into a satiny and glossy batter after a few minutes. Once the batter has become smooth, glossy, and can easily retain its shape, then it no longer needs any more eggs.

Transfer the choux dough to a piping bag fitted with an 829 French star piping tip. Pipe the choux dough onto the prepared baking sheet into little logs about 5 x 2 inches (13 x 5 cm) long and place them 3 inches (8 cm) apart. Dust the tops of the éclairs with the powdered sugar.

Bake the éclairs for 40 to 45 minutes. During the final 10 minutes of baking, poke two to three holes into the sides of the éclairs with a toothpick to help dry them out. Let the finished éclairs cool completely on a wire cooling rack before filling and decorating.

To make the Raspberry Glaze, cook the raspberries, lemon juice, lemon zest, cornstarch, and butter in a medium saucepan over medium heat. Bring the mixture to a low boil, stirring as the raspberries begin to break down. When the mixture begins to thicken, 6 to 8 minutes, remove the pan from the heat. Strain the berries through a fine-mesh sieve into a bowl, trapping all of the seeds. Cool the mixture to room temperature. To speed up this process, place the bowl into the fridge and stir every 10 minutes to dissipate the heat.

In a medium bowl, whisk together the Raspberry Glaze, almond extract, powdered sugar, and heavy cream until it becomes about the thickness of molasses.

Before assembling the éclairs, transfer the chilled Pistachio Pastry Cream to a piping bag fitted with a small round piping tip.

To assemble the éclairs. Poke three holes in the bottom of the éclairs with a small star-shaped piping tip. With the piping bag of Pistachio Pastry Cream, fill the inside of the éclair through these holes. Wipe off any excess cream that is poking out of the bottom.

Dip the tops of the éclairs into the Raspberry Glaze. Place the finished éclairs on a wire cooling rack placed over a baking sheet lined with parchment paper to catch any drips. Let the glaze partially harden before decorating the top with extra piped Pistachio Pastry Cream, fresh raspberries, and chopped pistachios. Serve the éclairs chilled.

To store the éclairs, keep them in the refrigerator covered for 3 to 4 days.

Raspberry Glaze

4 oz (113 g) fresh raspberries

1 tbsp (15 ml) fresh lemon juice

2 tsp (5 g) fresh lemon zest

1 tsp cornstarch

2 tbsp (29 g) salted butter

½ tsp almond extract

2 cups (236 g) powdered sugar

2 tbsp (30 ml) heavy cream

Fresh raspberries, for decorating

Chopped pistachios, for decorating

Dulce de Leche Cream Horns

There is nothing I quite enjoy as much as baking up a batch of cream horns. They always remind me of a little German-inspired bakery that I love to frequent in the summers. Elegantly wrapped, this pastry is much easier to recreate at home than it looks. This particular recipe is inspired by the enticingly rich flavor of dulce de leche cake. These cream horns look so beautiful served on an antique transferware plate!

First, make the Dulce de Leche Diplomat Cream. In a medium bowl, whisk together the egg yolks and sugar until the yolks have turned a pale yellow color and the mixture is thick and syrupy, about 4 minutes. Whisk in the cake flour and cornstarch.

In a medium saucepan, warm the milk and ½ cup (120 ml) of the heavy cream over medium-high heat until the liquid begins to just bubble at the edges of the pan. Be careful not to boil the milk and cream. Pour about 2 tablespoons (30 ml) of the cream mixture into the egg mixture and whisk, tempering the eggs. Then, pour all of the egg mixture into the pan of cream. Whisking the custard constantly, cook it over low heat until it thickens to a consistency that is thick, stiff, and smooth, similar to commercial mayonnaise. Continue to whisk for another 1 to 2 minutes after the custard has reached its peak thickness, and it will begin to become glossy and thin out slightly.

Remove the custard from the heat. With an immersion blender, or the custard can be transferred to a food processor, pulse the finished custard, butter, vanilla extract, and dulce de leche for 3 to 4 minutes, until it is thick and glossy. Cover the cream with plastic wrap that touches the surface of the cream. Place the cream into the refrigerator until fully chilled, about 3 hours.

Once the cream has finished chilling, whip the remaining ½ cup (120 ml) of heavy cream until it reaches stiff peaks, 5 to 6 minutes. Gently fold the whipped cream into the chilled Dulce de Leche Diplomat Cream, being careful not to deflate the whipped cream too much. Transfer the new diplomat cream to a piping bag fitted with a large star piping tip. Chill the cream until ready to use.

Preheat the oven to 425°F (218°C). Line a large baking sheet with parchment paper. Spray about 14 cream horn molds with cooking spray and set them aside.

(continued)

Makes about 14 cream horns

Dulce de Leche Diplomat Cream

2 large egg yolks

2 tbsp + 2 tsp (34 g) granulated sugar

1 tbsp (4 g) cake flour

1 tbsp (8 g) cornstarch

1 cup (240 ml) whole milk

1 cup (240 ml) heavy cream, divided

2 tbsp (29 g) salted butter, sliced

1 tsp vanilla extract

2 oz (56 g) dulce de leche

Cut the thawed puff pastry into about 14 long strips, about 1½ x 20 inches (4 x 51 cm). Beginning with the tapered end of the cream horn mold, begin wrapping the strip of puff pastry around the mold, overlapping the edges by about ¼ inch (6 mm). Continue wrapping until the pastry reaches the opposite end of the mold and pinch the seam closed. Repeat this with the remaining cream horns.

Arrange the cream horns on the prepared baking sheet, about 2 inches (5 cm) apart. Place the baking sheet into the refrigerator and chill the pastries for 20 to 25 minutes.

In a small bowl, whisk together the egg and water to make the egg wash. Brush the pastry all over with the egg wash. Sprinkle the pastries with the coarse sugar.

Bake the cream horns for 20 to 25 minutes, or until the pastry is golden brown and the inner layers are no longer doughy. Transfer the pastry still on the molds to a wire cooling rack. Let the pastry cool to room temperature before removing the molds; then allow the inside of the pastry to dry out a bit before filling, about 1 hour.

Once the pastry is ready to be filled, melt the chocolate chips in a microwave-safe dish. Dip the open ends of the cream horns into the chocolate and set them on a piece of parchment or wax paper to harden. When the chocolate has hardened, it is time to fill the cream horns. Pipe the Dulce de Leche Diplomat Cream into the cream horns until it peeks out from the inside. Keep the cream horns chilled until ready to serve, about 4 days.

Cream Horns

1 sheet (260 g) frozen puff pastry, thawed

1 egg + 1 tbsp (15 ml) water, for egg wash

2 tbsp (26 g) coarse sugar

½ cup (84 g) semisweet chocolate chips

Fanciful Pancakes, Waffles, and Donuts

Everyone deserves a romantic breakfast spread. Imagine waking up
to find the prettiest table covered in a lace tablecloth filled to the
brim with freshly made waffles and pancakes, biscuits with cream
and jam, cinnamon rolls and scones, plates of fresh fruit, warm maple
syrup, and piping hot coffee. Doesn't that sound divine? With these
beautiful breakfast bakes, we hope that you feel just as fancy
(as if that were true)!

In this chapter, you will be introduced to a lovely arrangement
of pretty pancakes of all kinds, savory waffles, and the prettiest
donuts. If you love living a life where cake is served for breakfast,
you will find that every recipe in this chapter will be welcome on
your table. Through the pages, you will find the loveliest treats, such
as Dark Chocolate Black Forest Pancakes (page 146) and Apple Cider
Donut Holes (page 159). If you love something fruity and floral, you
can whip up a batch of Rose Waffles with Strawberry Syrup (page 156)
or Individual Loaded Berry Dutch Babies (page 155). If you like a
savory breakfast, there is even a recipe for Belgian Waffle
Eggs Benedict (page 151)!

Fill up your breakfast tray with a few of these bakes, some fresh fruit,
and a piping hot pot of tea or coffee to enjoy while you read your
favorite historical drama or cozy fantasy novel. With each bite of
these fanciful breakfast treats, we hope they help you to snuggle in
for a cozy morning of relaxation in your own dreamy cottage.

Swedish Stacked Lemon Ricotta Pancakes

If you are in the mood for a cozy and comforting breakfast, you will love these Swedish pancakes. These pancakes are similar to crêpes, though they have a rustic charm that is uniquely Scandinavian. They are a tad thicker than the French-style crêpe, which makes them feel heartier. With this recipe, you will add a bright note of lemon and smooth, creamy ricotta cheese. Stack them high with layers of whipped lemon ricotta filling that makes them feel light as air. If you prefer, you may choose to simply fill them and roll them up to serve.

To make the Lemon Swedish Pancakes, in a blender or food processor, pulse together the flour, sugar, baking powder, and salt until well combined, 1 to 2 minutes.

Add the lightly beaten eggs, milk, lemon juice, lemon zest, vanilla, and melted butter. Pulse until the batter is smooth and has barely any lumps, about 2 minutes. Do not over mix the batter. Place the mixed batter into the fridge for at least 30 minutes before cooking the pancakes.

While the batter rests, make the Whipped Lemon Ricotta Cream. In a large bowl, whip the ricotta cheese with 2 tablespoons (30 g) of sugar until the cheese is thick and creamy, about 5 minutes. In a separate bowl, whip the heavy cream with the remaining 2 tablespoons (30 g) of sugar until it is thick and forms stiff peaks, 6 to 8 minutes. Fold the whipped ricotta cheese into the whipped cream along with the lemon juice and lemon zest. Cover the bowl with plastic wrap, and store it in the refrigerator until ready to use.

To cook the pancakes, warm a large skillet over medium-low heat. Brush the pan with butter or cooking spray and ladle ¼ cup (60 ml) of batter onto the hot skillet. Cook the pancakes on each side for 1 to 2 minutes, or until they are golden brown and cooked through. Stack them on a plate as they finish cooking and cover the plate with a towel to keep them warm.

To serve the pancakes as a stack, layer the pancakes with the Whipped Lemon Ricotta Cream in between the layers. Serve with fresh raspberries and maple syrup. Alternately, they can be rolled up like crêpes with the cream filling inside.

To store, keep the pancakes and filling separated in the refrigerator for about 4 days.

Makes about 16 pancakes

Lemon Swedish Pancakes

1½ cups (188 g) all-purpose flour

1 tbsp (15 g) granulated sugar

½ tsp baking powder

½ tsp kosher salt

2 large eggs, lightly beaten

2 cups (480 ml) whole milk

2 tbsp (30 ml) fresh lemon juice

1 tbsp (7 g) lemon zest

1 tsp vanilla extract

¼ cup (60 ml) melted salted butter

Whipped Lemon Ricotta Cream

½ cup (120 ml) ricotta cheese

¼ cup (60 g) granulated sugar, divided

½ cup (120 ml) heavy cream

2 tbsp (15 ml) fresh lemon juice

2 tbsp (15 g) lemon zest

Fresh raspberries, for serving

Maple syrup, for serving

Dark Chocolate Black Forest Pancakes

Inspired by the rural charm of the German countryside, the Black Forest cake comes from the Black Forest region. The cake is a decadently rich dessert with layers of chocolate sponge cake, whipped cream, and cherries. Now, imagine waking up to a plate full of positively sumptuous dark chocolate pancakes topped with a warm cherry compote and fluffy whipped cream! If you are a fan of the cake, then you will love the memorable flavors of luscious chocolate and juicy cherries that make this a truly unique breakfast!

In a medium saucepan, begin by making the Cherry Compote. Bring the cherries, sugar, lemon juice, and cherry liqueur (if using) to a boil over medium heat. Lower the heat to a simmer and stir occasionally, until the fruit breaks down and the sauce thickens slightly, about 10 minutes. Remove the pot from the heat and transfer the compote to a bowl. Cover the bowl with plastic wrap and let the compote rest.

Next, make the Whipped Cream. In a large bowl or a standing electric mixer fitted with a whisk, beat the heavy cream and sugar together until the cream forms stiff peaks, 5 to 6 minutes. Cover the bowl and keep the Whipped Cream refrigerated until ready to use. If you prefer, the Whipped Cream can be transferred to a piping bag fitted with a star tip for a more decorative look!

To begin making the Dark Chocolate Pancakes, in a large bowl, whisk together the flour, cocoa powder, sugar, baking powder, and salt. Add the egg, melted butter, melted dark chocolate, and buttermilk and stir until everything is just combined and there are no visible lumps in the batter, 3 to 4 minutes.

Heat a griddle or skillet over the stove to around 375°F (191°C). Spray the griddle with cooking spray or a small pat of butter. Cook the pancakes for 2 to 3 minutes on the first side, then for 1 to 2 minutes on the opposite side, or until they are cooked through the middle and no longer soupy.

Store the pancakes on a plate covered with a warm towel as you cook the remaining pancakes.

To serve the pancakes, layer them with the warm Cherry Compote and Whipped Cream. For a decorative look, use extra fresh cherries on top. Don't forget a little drizzle of maple syrup!

To store the pancakes, keep the components separated in the refrigerator for about 4 days.

Makes about 12 pancakes

Cherry Compote

1 cup (140 g) fresh sweet cherries, pitted and halved

½ cup (100 g) granulated sugar

1 tbsp (15 ml) fresh lemon juice

1 tbsp (15 ml) cherry liqueur, optional

Whipped Cream

1 cup (240 ml) heavy cream

¼ cup (50 g) granulated sugar

Dark Chocolate Pancakes

1 cup (125 g) all-purpose flour

2 tbsp (12 g) Dutch cocoa powder

2 tbsp (30 g) granulated sugar

2 tsp (9 g) baking powder

½ tsp kosher salt

1 large egg

2 tbsp (30 ml) melted salted butter

1 oz (28 g) melted dark chocolate, slightly cooled

¾ cup (180 ml) buttermilk

Fresh whole cherries, for serving

Maple syrup, for serving

Blueberry Mascarpone Stuffed Crêpes

Stuffed crêpes may be the prettiest breakfast I have ever laid eyes on! These delicate French-style crêpes are simply divine, especially when filled with the dreamiest Blueberry Mascarpone Cream. There are many ways to serve these crêpes, but my personal favorite is to fold them into sweet little triangles, with the lovely purple-blue filling peeking out. Of course, you can't forget to add a generous helping of fresh berries and maybe even a few sprigs of mint for a touch of garden-fresh goodness. This light and fluffy breakfast treat is simply perfect for a cozy summer morning in the countryside!

To make the Blueberry Mascarpone Cream, begin by making a blueberry syrup over the stove. In a small saucepan, bring the blueberries, lemon juice, and sugar to a boil over medium heat. Lower the heat to a simmer and stir constantly, until the berries have burst and the sauce has started to thicken slightly, about 10 minutes. Remove the pan from the heat and let the syrup cool for 10 to 15 minutes.

Meanwhile, bring another small pan of water to a boil and place a small bowl over the pan without touching the water. Melt the chocolate and butter in the bowl, stirring constantly until the chocolate is no longer lumpy. Remove the bowl from over the water and set this aside to cool for about 5 to 6 minutes.

In a large bowl, cream the mascarpone until it is smooth. Stir in the blueberry syrup, white chocolate and butter mixture, vanilla, and salt. In a separate bowl, whip the heavy cream until it reaches stiff peaks, 3 to 4 minutes. Gently fold the whipped cream into the mascarpone filling. Cover the bowl with plastic wrap and refrigerate until ready to use.

Makes about 9 crêpes

Blueberry Mascarpone Cream

½ cup (68 g) fresh blueberries

1 tbsp (15 ml) fresh lemon juice

¼ cup (50 g) granulated sugar

½ cup (84 g) white chocolate chips

1 tbsp (14 g) salted butter

8 oz (226 g) mascarpone, softened

1 tsp vanilla extract

Pinch of kosher salt

½ cup (120 ml) heavy cream

(continued)

To make the Classic French Crêpes, combine the flour, ¼ cup (60 ml) of the milk, the sugar, salt, beaten eggs, and melted butter in a large bowl. Whisk until there are no visible lumps in the batter, 3 to 4 minutes. Then, add in the remaining 1¼ cups (300 ml) of milk to the batter and it will be very thin. Cover the bowl with a tea towel and let the batter rest for about 30 minutes before cooking the crêpes.

In a 10.5-inch (27-cm) skillet over medium-high heat, spread a thin layer of coconut or canola oil. This is best done with a paper towel, if possible, so that the oil is very thin. When the pan begins to smoke slightly, it is hot enough to cook the crêpes. Scoop about ¼ cup (60 ml) of batter into the corner of the pan and spread it around to the edges by tilting the pan; then spread it into the center of the pan adding any extra batter to fill in holes. Cook the crêpe for 40 to 60 seconds or until the edges begin to turn golden brown. With a thin metal spatula or your fingertips, flip the crêpe over. Cook on the opposite side for another 30 seconds.

Place the finished crêpe on a plate and cover it with a warm towel while you cook the remaining batter.

To serve the crêpes, fill them with a healthy dollop of Blueberry Mascarpone Cream. Fold the crêpes in half, then in half again, to create a triangle shape. Otherwise, they can be rolled like a burrito. Serve the crêpes warm with any extra Blueberry Mascarpone Cream, maple syrup, fresh blueberries, and sprigs of fresh mint on top.

To store the crêpe filling, keep it in the refrigerator in an airtight container for about 5 days. The crêpes do not store well, so they should be eaten right away!

Classic French Crêpes

1 cup (125 g) all-purpose flour

1½ cups (360 ml) whole milk, divided

2 tbsp (30 g) granulated sugar

Pinch of kosher salt

2 large eggs, beaten

2 tbsp (30 ml) melted salted butter

Coconut or canola oil, for cooking crêpes

Maple syrup, for serving

Fresh blueberries, for serving

Fresh mint leaves, for serving

Belgian Waffle Eggs Benedict

A true Belgian waffle is made with yeast and has whipped egg whites folded into the batter, creating a super soft and puffy waffle. This batter takes a few more steps than the traditional waffle, but the results are pure magic! Because this waffle is not as sweet, it makes an excellent base for Eggs Benedict. Topped with Canadian bacon, a poached egg, and the creamiest Hollandaise sauce, this will be your new favorite breakfast. This dish looks beautiful served at brunch with your prettiest dishes and fresh flowers picked from the garden or from the farmers' market!

Begin by making the Hollandaise Sauce. Cut the butter into pieces and, in a small saucepan, melt the butter. Remove the pan from the heat and set this aside.

In a medium saucepan, whisk the egg yolks until they are thick and syrupy, about 2 minutes. Whip in the lemon juice and salt, beating for another 1 minute. Add the cold butter and place the pan over low heat. Whisk the egg yolks with a wire whisk until they begin to thicken, about 2 minutes. When the yolks begin to look like custard on the tines of the whisk, it has thickened enough.

Remove the pan from the heat and beat in the Dijon mustard and paprika. Then, slowly begin to add the previously melted butter, ¼ teaspoon at a time, whisking all the while. The sauce will begin to thicken the more butter that you add. As the sauce thickens and emulsifies into a cream-like consistency, the melted butter can then be added in a slow and steady stream as you continue to whisk. Try to add as much of the butter as possible until the sauce is thickened to your liking. Once the sauce has been made, you will want to keep it warm so that it does not begin to separate; place the sauce pan, covered, in a pan with a few inches of lukewarm water.

To make the Belgian Waffles, begin by whisking together the flour, yeast, and salt. Then, add the melted butter, milk, and 3 egg yolks. Stir until the batter is no longer lumpy, 2 to 4 minutes.

Meanwhile, in a separate large bowl, beat the 3 egg whites until they are foamy and reach soft peaks, or the tips curl, 3 to 4 minutes. Slowly add the sugar, about 1 tablespoon (15 g) at a time, until the whites reach stiff peaks, or the tips stand straight up, about 5 minutes. Gently fold in half of the stiffened egg whites into the waffles batter fully mixing it in. Then, fold in the second half of the egg whites to the batter until it is fully mixed in, about 4 minutes total.

(continued)

Makes about 8 waffles

Hollandaise Sauce

1½ cups (348 g) unsalted butter

3 egg yolks

1 tbsp (15 ml) lemon juice

¼ tsp kosher salt

1 tbsp (14 g) cold, unsalted butter

1 tsp Dijon mustard

Pinch of paprika

Belgian Waffles

2 cups (250 g) all-purpose flour

1 tsp active dry yeast

½ tsp kosher salt

¼ cup (58 g) melted salted butter, slightly cooled

1¾ cups (420 ml) whole milk

3 large eggs, separated

3 tbsp (45 g) granulated sugar

Preheat a waffle iron and spray it liberally with cooking spray. Spread the waffle batter evenly and cook the waffles for 5 to 6 minutes or according to the directions for your waffle maker. Place the finished waffles on a plate and cover with a warm towel to keep them warm. If necessary, they can be placed in a 170°F (77°C) oven to keep them warm while you make the eggs.

To poach the eggs, begin with a large pot of about 2 quarts (2 L) of water. Bring the water to a simmer at about 180 to 190°F (82 to 88°C).

Place a fine-mesh sieve over a small bowl. Very gently crack the egg into the sieve. With a gentle hand, swirl the egg around in the sieve, letting any of the loose and watery egg white fall through into the bowl underneath. What should be left is the yolk and the tightest part of the white. Meanwhile, set aside a medium bowl of warm water for later.

With the sieve, tip the remaining egg into the simmering water. Swirl the water around in a small vortex until the egg begins to set, 10 to 20 seconds. Let the egg continue to cook until the whites are fully set, about 4 minutes.

With a slotted spoon, remove the poached egg from the water and place it into the bowl of warm water. Leave the egg in the warm water while you cook the remaining eggs to keep it warm.

To serve the waffles, stack the waffles with two pieces of warm Canadian bacon, a poached egg, and drizzle on the Hollandaise Sauce. Top with flaky sea salt, freshly cracked pepper, and chopped chives for garnish.

To store the waffles, keep the leftovers in an airtight container in the refrigerator for up to 4 days. The Hollandaise Sauce may be kept in an airtight container in the refrigerator for 2 to 3 days, and reheated in a double boiler; do not reheat in the microwave or it will overcook the eggs. To store the poached eggs, keep them in an airtight container in the refrigerator for about 3 days; to reheat, place them into a bowl of hot water until warmed to your liking.

Poached Eggs

8 large eggs

1 tsp white distilled vinegar

16 slices Canadian bacon

Flaky sea salt, for serving

Freshly cracked pepper, for serving

Chopped chives, for garnish

Individual Loaded Berry Dutch Babies

On pleasant summer mornings, one of my favorite breakfasts is a puffy German pancake, otherwise known as a Dutch baby. These pancakes are baked in a hot skillet, rising to incredible heights in the oven, only to sink back down again after they are delivered to the table. While many recipes are baking in a large skillet, this recipe is baked in miniature skillets so that everyone may enjoy their own Dutch baby! Dress it up however you like, sweet or savory, but for this version, they are loaded with fresh summer berries and whipped cream. Yum!

Preheat the oven to 450°F (232°C). Place eight 4-inch (10-cm) cast-iron skillets into the oven and let them preheat for at least 30 minutes.

In a blender or food processor, blend together the eggs, 2 tablespoons (29 g) of the butter, the milk, flour, sugar, cinnamon, nutmeg, salt, and vanilla until there are no lumps in the batter, 2 to 3 minutes.

Once the skillets are nice and hot, divide the remaining 4 tablespoons (58 g) of butter between the eight skillets, letting it melt fully. Immediately pour the batter into the skillets, filling them three-quarters of the way full, dividing it as evenly as possible. Place the skillets back into the oven and bake for 15 to 18 minutes, or until the pancakes have puffed and turned golden brown. Lower the oven temperature to 350°F (177°C) and bake for another 5 minutes. Alternately, you can bake all of the batter in one 10-inch (25-cm) skillet for 18 to 20 minutes, followed by another 5 minutes at 350°F (177°C).

Remove the Dutch babies from the oven and top with the fresh berries. Serve them hot alongside freshly whipped cream and maple syrup.

To store your Dutch babies, wrap them in plastic wrap or place in an airtight container in the refrigerator for about 4 days.

Makes 8 (4-inch [10-cm]) pancakes

4 large eggs

6 tbsp (87 g) salted butter, softened and divided

1 cup (240 ml) whole milk

1 cup (125 g) all-purpose flour

1 tbsp (15 g) granulated sugar

½ tsp ground cinnamon

¼ tsp ground nutmeg

Pinch of kosher salt

1 tsp vanilla extract

2 cups (300 g) various berries, such as strawberries, blueberries, and blackberries

Whipped cream, for serving

Maple syrup, for serving

Rose Waffles with Strawberry Syrup

Have you ever thought of using the essence of roses in your baking? Rose petals have many wonderful benefits to your health, and they add such a unique flavor to baked goods. In this recipe, you will use rose-infused water to flavor your waffles. While the rose water does not give these waffles a super bright pink coloring, you can supplement this with a bit of pink food coloring, if desired. This waffle recipe is paired with a Strawberry Simple Syrup that truly brings out the floral flavor! These waffles look as if they were made for a fantasy breakfast!

Begin by making the Rose Water. In a small saucepan, bring the water to a boil. Stir in the rose petals and lower the heat to a simmer. Cover the pot with a lid and simmer the water for about 30 minutes, or until the rose petals have wilted and lost their color entirely. Remove the pot from the heat and let the water cool completely. Strain the water through a mesh sieve, reserving the water for use later. Discard or compost the rose petals.

To make the Rose Waffles, whisk together the flour, sugar, baking powder, and salt in a large bowl. Add the eggs, melted butter, heavy cream, rose water, vanilla, and food coloring (if using) and whisk until the batter is smooth and has hardly any lumps in it, 2 to 3 minutes. Let the batter rest on the counter for about 30 minutes.

While the batter rests, make the Strawberry Simple Syrup. In a small saucepan, bring the water to a boil. Whisk in the sugar, dissolving it. Then add in the strawberries. Reduce the heat to a simmer and cook the syrup until the strawberries begin to break down, 10 to 15 minutes. The syrup can be served warm or chilled, depending on your preference.

Preheat a waffle iron and spray with cooking spray. Cook the waffles for 4 to 5 minutes or according to the directions for your waffle maker. Continue with the remaining batter, making about 12 waffles.

Serve the waffles with whipped cream, fresh rosebuds and petals, fresh strawberries, and a heavy drizzle of Strawberry Simple Syrup! Store your waffles and syrup in airtight containers in the refrigerator for up to 5 days.

Makes about 12 waffles

Rose Water

1 cup (240 ml) water

¾ cup (66 g) fresh food-grade rose petals (see Tip)

Rose Waffles

2 cups (250 g) all-purpose flour

¼ cup (50 g) granulated sugar

4 tsp (18 g) baking powder

¼ tsp kosher salt

2 large eggs

½ cup (120 ml) melted salted butter

½ cup (120 ml) heavy cream

¾ cup (180 ml) rose water

1 tsp vanilla extract

Pink or red food coloring, optional

Strawberry Simple Syrup

1 cup (240 ml) water

2 cups (400 g) granulated sugar

4 oz (113 g) fresh strawberries, quartered

Whipped cream, for serving

Fresh rosebuds and petals, for serving

Fresh strawberries, for serving

Tip
If you do not have access to fresh food-grade rose petals, you can purchase premade rose water online!

Apple Cider Donut Holes

Oh, there is nothing quite so comforting as apple cider donuts in the fall! They evoke memories of meandering through apple orchards and handpicking apples on lazy weekends with my family. Just the aroma itself has the power to transport me to a place of joy and nostalgia! Do you have similar blissful memories from autumns past? These delightful donut holes are more cake-like than others, spiced perfectly and infused with an apple cider reduction. They are so cute served in little cups with parchment paper!

Begin by making the donut batter. In a small saucepan, bring the apple cider to a boil. Lower the heat to a simmer and reduce the apple cider until there is ½ cup (120 ml) of thick, syrupy apple cider left. Let the apple cider reduction cool to room temperature before using it in the batter.

In a large bowl, whisk together the flour, sugar, baking powder, cinnamon, pumpkin pie spice, and salt. Add in the egg, milk, vanilla, melted butter, and the apple cider reduction. Mix well until the batter is thick and a bit puffy. Set this aside.

Meanwhile, make the Cinnamon Sugar Coating. In a medium bowl, combine the sugar and cinnamon until well blended. Set this aside.

In a large, heavy-bottomed pot or deep fryer, heat the canola oil to 375°F (191°C). Using a small cookie scoop, drop the batter into the hot oil. Fry the donut holes for about 4 minutes, or until they are dark brown in color and fluffy in the center, flipping them halfway through cooking. Remove the donut holes with a slotted spoon and place them on a wire cooling rack situated over a baking sheet. When the donut holes are still hot but cool enough to handle, roll them in the cinnamon sugar.

Continue frying the remaining batter and coating the donut holes in the cinnamon sugar. Serve the donut holes hot. Store the finished donuts at room temperature in an airtight container for about 4 days.

Makes about 24 donut holes

Apple Cider Donut Holes

1 cup (240 ml) apple cider

2 cups (250 g) all-purpose flour

¼ cup (50 g) granulated sugar

1½ tsp (7 g) baking powder

1 tsp ground cinnamon

1 tsp pumpkin pie spice

½ tsp kosher salt

1 large egg

½ cup (120 ml) whole milk

1 tsp vanilla extract

¼ cup (60 ml) melted salted butter

3 quarts (2.8 L) canola oil

Cinnamon Sugar Coating

1 cup (200 g) granulated sugar

1 tbsp (8 g) ground cinnamon

Dirty Chai Latte Filled Donuts

Imagine your cozy cottage with a warm fire crackling in the wood stove and the scent of freshly baked donuts filling the room. With your favorite fantasy novel in hand and the table decorated with collected autumn leaves and pinecones from your nature walk, what could be more perfect for such a day as a batch of spiced donuts inspired by a dirty chai latte? Coated in Chai-Spiced Sugar and filled with Dirty Chai Cream, you can taste the essence of chai and a shot of espresso with every bite.

Begin by making the Dirty Chai Cream filling. In a large bowl, whisk together the egg yolks and sugar until the eggs turn pale yellow and the mixture becomes thick and syrupy, about 4 minutes. Whisk in the salt, cornstarch, instant espresso powder, cinnamon, ginger, cloves, allspice, nutmeg, and cardamom. Set this aside.

In a medium saucepan over medium heat, warm the milk until the edges of the pan just begin to simmer. Remove the pan from the heat and pour about 2 tablespoons (30 ml) of the warm milk into the egg mixture. Immediately whisk the warm milk into the egg mixture to temper the eggs, then pour the entire egg mixture into the pan of warm milk. Return the pan to low heat and whisk constantly, until the cream begins to thicken. Continue to whisk constantly until the custard becomes thick, creamy, and glossy like commercial mayonnaise, 5 to 6 minutes. Once the custard has reached its peak thickness, whisk another 1 to 2 minutes, and the custard will thin slightly and look satiny.

Remove the pan from the heat and pulse in the butter and vanilla with an immersion blender, or transfer to a food processor, until the butter has melted, 1 to 2 minutes. Cover the custard with plastic wrap touching the surface of the custard and place it in the refrigerator. Allow the custard to chill completely, about 3 hours.

Once the custard has chilled, make the whipped cream. Whip the heavy cream until it reaches stiff peaks, 3 to 4 minutes. Gently fold the whipped cream into the chilled custard, creating a light and fluffy diplomat cream. Transfer the cream to a piping bag fitted with a large star piping tip. Store the cream in the refrigerator until ready to use. Alternately, this cream can be made a day or two ahead.

(continued)

Makes 14 to 16 donuts

Dirty Chai Cream

2 egg yolks

3 tbsp (45 g) granulated sugar

¼ tsp kosher salt

1½ tbsp (12 g) cornstarch

1 tsp instant espresso powder

½ tsp ground cinnamon

½ tsp ground ginger

¼ tsp ground cloves

¼ tsp ground allspice

¼ tsp ground nutmeg

Pinch of ground cardamom

1 cup (240 ml) whole milk

1½ tbsp (22 g) salted butter, sliced

1½ tsp (8 ml) vanilla extract

½ cup (120 ml) heavy cream

Dirty Chai Latte Filled Donuts *(continued)*

Next, make the Chai-Spiced Sugar. In a large flat dish, such as a pie pan, whisk together the sugar, cinnamon, ginger, cloves, allspice, nutmeg, and cardamom. Set this aside.

To make the Spiced Donuts, begin by mixing together 2 cups (250 g) of the flour, the yeast, salt, cinnamon, and nutmeg in a large electric mixer fitted with a dough hook. Grease a large bowl and set it aside.

In a small saucepan over medium heat, warm the sugar and milk together to about 110°F (43°C). Add the warm milk mixture to the flour mixture, along with the butter, eggs, and vanilla. Whisk until everything is well blended, about 2 minutes.

Slowly begin to incorporate the remaining flour, 1 cup (125 g) at a time, until a soft dough forms. Knead the dough for 3 to 4 minutes on medium speed after all of the flour has been added. This dough will be sticky and very soft.

Bring the dough out onto the countertop and shape it into a ball. It helps to have wet hands or use a bench scraper, as the dough is very sticky. Place the dough into the greased bowl and cover it with plastic wrap or a damp kitchen towel. Let the dough rise until doubled, about 1 hour.

After the dough has doubled, gently deflate it with your hands. Roll the dough out about ½ inch (1.3 cm) thick. Cut out the dough with a 3-inch (8-cm) biscuit cutter. Place the donuts on a well-floured surface in a warm place and cover them with plastic wrap or a damp kitchen towel. Let the donuts puff slightly, 20 to 25 minutes.

Place two large baking sheets lined with parchment paper on your countertop. In a heavy-bottomed pot or a deep fryer, heat the canola oil to 375°F (191°C). Working in batches of three or four donuts, fry the donuts, risen side down, in the oil for about 2 minutes per side. The donuts are finished when they are golden brown on the outside and the inside is no longer doughy.

Chai-Spiced Sugar

1 cup (200 g) granulated sugar

1 tsp ground cinnamon

1 tsp ground ginger

½ tsp ground cloves

¼ tsp ground allspice

¼ tsp ground nutmeg

¼ tsp ground cardamom

Spiced Donuts

5 cups (625 g) all-purpose flour, divided, plus more for dusting

1 tbsp (12 g) active dry yeast

½ tsp kosher salt

1 tsp ground cinnamon

¼ tsp ground nutmeg

⅓ cup (66 g) granulated sugar

1¼ cups (300 ml) whole milk

¼ cup (58 g) salted butter, softened

2 large eggs

1 tsp vanilla extract

3 quarts (2 L) canola oil

Place the finished donuts onto the prepared baking sheets. When they are still warm but not too hot to handle with your fingers, roll the donuts gently in the Chai Spiced Sugar and place them back on the baking sheets to rest until they reach room temperature.

After all of the donuts have been fried, it is time to fill them. Using a chopstick or the end of a thin wooden spoon, poke a hole on the side of the donut. Gently press it around the inside to create a cavity for the filling.

Pipe the Dirty Chai Cream filling into the hole you just made in the donut. Pipe slowly, pulling the bag away from the donut as you fill it. For decorative purposes, you can let a little cream poke out of the side, or pipe a little decorative design around the opening. Serve the donuts at room temperature. Store the finished donuts in the refrigerator in an airtight container for 3 to 4 days.

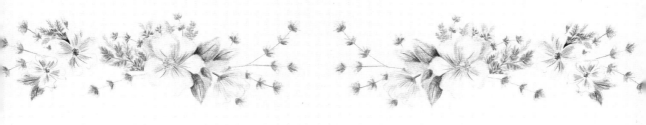

Old-Fashioned Desserts

There is something so lovely and cozy about an old-fashioned style dessert. These are the desserts that you will find inside your grandma's old community cookbook with tattered and yellow pages, stained from being used so often. You may not see many of these confections on the menu at your local café nor on the pages of many modern cookbooks, but these are the sweet treats that you have seen before at a local potluck or on your family's holiday buffet table. Though many of these pretty desserts are beginning to disappear from our weekly baking, I say it is time to bring them back!

From Personal Clementine Pavlovas (page 182) to Biscuit-Topped Blackberry Cobbler (page 181) and Strawberry Apricot Basque Cheesecake (page 168), you will find that these desserts are anything but old! This collection of granny's favorites is beautifully flavored, soft and creamy, and absolutely gorgeous from head to toe. These recipes have an inspired modern twist, giving them a depth and flavor that is out of this world tasty. This is, in my opinion, the best chapter of this little cookbook. You will not be disappointed by the delightfulness inside!

Sea Salt Butterscotch Pots de Crème

As the leaves begin to turn colors and the crisp autumn air fills the countryside, it feels only right to indulge in a luscious custard dessert flavored with caramel. On the stovetop sits a pot of creamy butterscotch custard, ready to be baked in the oven. This dessert is a French culinary classic that dates back to the 1600s. The slow cooking method of this custard creates a lovely, supple cream that is positively delicate. Serve in little glass jars or ramekins and top with a dollop of whipped cream and a sprinkling of flaky sea salt to savor the simple pleasures of autumn.

Preheat the oven to 325°F (163°C). Warm a pot of water on the stove until it begins to steam and pour the water into a 9 x 13–inch (22 x 33–cm) baking dish. Place the baking dish near the oven to keep it warm but not boiling. Set six 4-inch (10-cm) ramekins or glass jars in the warm water.

In a medium saucepan over medium heat, melt the butter. Whisk in the brown sugar and ½ cup (120 ml) of the heavy cream, cooking over medium heat until the sugar is dissolved. Bring to a gentle boil and cook for a further 5 minutes, until the caramel reaches 220°F (104°C) on a candy thermometer. Remove the pot from the heat and let it cool for about 10 minutes.

In a medium bowl, whisk together the egg yolks and granulated sugar until the yolks are pale yellow and the mixture is thick and syrupy, 3 to 4 minutes.

To the saucepan of caramel sauce, pour in the remaining 1½ cups (360 ml) of heavy cream and the milk. Put the pan over medium heat and warm the caramel mixture until the edges just begin to simmer, and the caramel has fully melted. Pour about 2 tablespoons (30 ml) of the caramel mixture into the eggs, whisking to temper the eggs. Then, pour all of the egg mixture into the caramel mixture and warm it over medium-low heat until it thickens just slightly, 3 to 4 minutes.

Remove the pan from the heat and immediately pour the custard into the ramekins. Cover each of the ramekins with a small piece of tin foil. Place the entire pan of water and the ramekins into the preheated oven and bake them for 40 to 45 minutes, or until they are set around the edges but jiggly in the center. Remove the foil, place the pan on a wire cooling rack, and cool for 25 to 30 minutes. Remove the ramekins from the water and place the ramekins into the refrigerator and chill fully, about 3 hours.

Serve the custard chilled topped with whipped cream and flaky sea salt. Store the finished custard covered in the refrigerator for about 4 days.

Makes about 6 custards

2 tbsp (29 g) salted butter, sliced

1 cup (194 g) light brown sugar, packed

2 cups (480 ml) heavy cream, divided

6 egg yolks

¼ cup (50 g) granulated sugar

¾ cup (160 ml) whole milk

Whipped cream, for serving

Flaky sea salt, for serving

Strawberry Apricot Basque Cheesecake

As the sweet scents of late spring and early summer blooms fill the air, there is nothing quite like delighting in the divine combination of juicy apricots and freshly picked strawberries. The pairing of these two summer fruits in a sweet compote is made even sweeter by serving it atop a creamy Basque cheesecake. This dessert hails from Spain and is lovingly crafted with a "burnt" top and rich, custard-like center.

Preheat the oven to 400°F (204°C). Place a 10-inch (25-cm) springform pan on a large baking sheet. Spray the pan with cooking spray, then line the pan with parchment paper so that it sticks up all the way around the edges of the pan. Set this aside while you prepare the cheesecake.

In a large bowl, cream together the cream cheese, mascarpone, sugar, and eggs, adding the eggs one at a time, waiting for each to become incorporated before adding the next, 6 to 8 minutes total. Whisk in the flour, salt, vanilla, heavy cream, and lemon zest until the batter is consistent and smooth, 2 to 3 minutes.

Pour the batter into the prepared pan and place the pan and baking sheet into the fridge for about 30 minutes. After chilling, bake the cheesecake for 45 to 50 minutes, or until the top is generously browned and the center is jiggly like Jell-O. Bring the cheesecake onto the counter to cool for about 1 hour, then refrigerate the cake for 8 to 10 hours or overnight.

To make the Strawberry Apricot Compote, bring the strawberries, apricots, sugar, lemon juice, and lemon zest to a boil over the stove in a medium-sized saucepan. Lower the heat to a simmer and cook the compote until the fruit begins to break down and the sauce thickens slightly, about 10 minutes. Set the compote aside to cool slightly before pouring it over the cheesecake.

When the cheesecake has chilled, remove it from the pan. Remove the springform pan's sides and gently unwrap the parchment from the sides of the cheesecake. It is okay if it is irregularly shaped—that is the charm of the cake! Serve the cake sliced with a heavy scoop of Strawberry Apricot Compote.

To store the cheesecake, cover with plastic wrap or place in airtight container and keep in the refrigerator for up to 5 days.

Makes 1 (10-inch [25-cm]) cheesecake

Mascarpone Basque Cheesecake

1¾ lbs (670 g) cream cheese, softened

8 oz (226 g) mascarpone, softened

2 cups (400 g) granulated sugar

7 large eggs

1 tbsp (8 g) all-purpose flour

½ tsp kosher salt

1 tsp vanilla extract

1 cup (240 ml) heavy cream

1 tsp fresh lemon zest

Strawberry Apricot Compote

10 oz (283 g) fresh strawberries, quartered

10 oz (283 g) fresh apricots, peeled and sliced

⅓ cup (66 g) granulated sugar

1 tbsp (15 ml) fresh lemon juice

1 tsp fresh lemon zest

Layered Blueberry No-Bake Cheesecakes

After a day spent gathering blueberries, you may be in search of a charming confection to prepare! These dainty ombré blueberry cheesecakes are divine, with their airy texture, tart flavor, and adorable appearance. They are a breeze to whip up, requiring only a touch of artistry to achieve their final whimsical look. The no-bake cheesecake became popular in the mid 1960s with Jell-O as the main ingredient. This recipe adds the charm of utilizing from-scratch elements and an enchanting presentation to give a tribute to this vintage dessert.

Begin by making the Blueberry Syrup. In a food processor or blender, pulse the blueberries until they are smooth and fully pureed, 2 to 3 minutes. Transfer the pureed blueberries to a medium saucepan and add the lemon juice and sugar. Place the saucepan over medium-high heat and bring the fruit to a boil, then lower the heat to a simmer. Simmer and stir the blueberries until the sugar dissolves and the syrup begins to thicken slightly, about 10 minutes.

Once the syrup has thickened to the consistency of maple syrup, remove the pan from the heat and pour the syrup through a fine-mesh sieve situated over a bowl. Let the syrup drain, collecting the blueberry pulp in the sieve. Press out as much of the syrup as possible with a silicone spatula. Cover the syrup with plastic wrap and let the syrup cool to room temperature before using.

Meanwhile, make the Graham Cracker Crust. In a large bowl, mix together the graham cracker crumbs, sugar, and melted butter until it becomes well saturated, 1 to 2 minutes. You may have to break apart any large clumps so that all of the crumbs are uniform.

Once the crust has come together, you will want to press it into the molds. In my personal experience, I used cake collars cut and taped into 2½-inch (6-cm) circles to make this recipe. If you do not have cake collars, you can use a mini cheesecake pan or a muffin tin, though the latter may have an inverted cone shape. Place the cake collars, if using, on a baking sheet. Divide the Graham Cracker Crust evenly between eight mini cheesecakes, about ¼ cup (42 g) of crust. Place the baking sheet or cheesecake pan into the refrigerator for at least 30 minutes.

(continued)

Makes 8 mini cheesecakes

Blueberry Syrup
1 cup (148 g) fresh blueberries

2 tbsp (30 ml) fresh lemon juice

½ cup (100 g) granulated sugar

Graham Cracker Crust
2 cups (228 g) graham cracker crumbs

⅓ cup (66 g) granulated sugar

½ cup (120 ml) melted salted butter

While the crust is chilling, make the No-Bake Cheesecake Filling. In a large bowl, cream together the cream cheese, sour cream, granulated sugar, powdered sugar, and vanilla until smooth, and there are no visible lumps of cream cheese, 5 to 6 minutes.

In a separate large bowl, whip the heavy cream until it reaches stiff peaks, 3 to 4 minutes. Gently fold one half of the whipped cream into the cream cheese mixture, then fold in the second half, until it is light and fluffy, 4 to 5 minutes total.

Divide the cheesecake filling among three medium bowls. With the Blueberry Syrup, use about two-thirds of the mix in one of the bowls of cheesecake filling. This will be the top and darkest layer. Divide the remaining one-third of the blueberry mixture between the other two bowls of cheesecake filling, making one a medium shade of blue and the other a very light shade of blue. It will take a bit of experimenting and mixing to get the shades that you want as the cheesecake filling really drinks up the Blueberry Syrup after sitting for a minute or two.

Once the fillings have been colored to your liking, it is time to layer them. Bring the chilled crusts to the countertop. Scoop the different colored fillings into three piping bags with the tips cut off. Pipe the lightest colored layer into the cheesecakes, directly over the Graham Cracker Crust. Smooth out any air bubbles with the back of a spoon. Then, pipe the medium-colored layer over the lightest colored layer. Smooth out any air bubbles again. Finally, finish with the darkest colored layer, smoothing out any air bubbles and smoothing out the top of the cheesecake as best as you can.

Place the cheesecakes into the freezer for several hours or until the cheesecakes are fully hardened and no longer super jiggly. Once they have been chilled and hardened, cut them out of the cake collars or pop them out of the cheesecake pan with a knife. Decorate the tops of the cheesecakes with fresh blueberries, whipped cream, and drizzled white chocolate. Edible flowers make for a wonderful touch, as well! Serve the cheesecakes chilled.

To store the cheesecakes, cover them with foil and place in the refrigerator for up to 4 to 5 days.

No-Bake Cheesecake Filling

1½ cups (348 g) cream cheese, softened

¼ cup (60 ml) sour cream, room temperature

½ cup (100 g) granulated sugar

⅔ cup (79 g) powdered sugar

1 tsp vanilla extract

1½ cups (360 ml) heavy cream

Blueberries, for decorating

Extra whipped cream, for decorating

Melted white chocolate, for decorating

Edible flowers, for decorating

Sticky Toffee Pear Puddings

A rich and decadent English dessert, sticky toffee pudding or sticky date pudding was created sometime in the early 20th century. With the same base as a fluffy sponge cake, the batter itself is made with rich ingredients like brown sugar, cinnamon, nutmeg, ginger, and cardamom, combined with soaked dates and espresso. This version includes Brown Sugar–Poached Pears and is topped with a delicious, sticky toffee caramel sauce, making this an incredibly luscious dessert. What's even better? It's made in individual servings, which creates a memorable presentation.

To begin, place the chopped dates and raisins in a small bowl. Cover the dried fruit with the boiling water and stir to completely cover the dates and raisins. Allow the fruit to soak in the hot water for 1 hour.

While you wait, you may begin making the Brown Sugar—Poached Pears. Peel the pears completely but leave them whole. In a large saucepan, bring the water and brown sugar to a boil, whisking constantly to dissolve the sugar. Add the pears and vanilla and lower the heat to a simmer. Simmer the pears in the syrup for about 20 minutes, turning them over occasionally. Remove the pan from the heat and let the pears cool to room temperature.

Preheat the oven to 350°F (177°C). Grease and flour six 8-ounce (226-g) ramekins. Place the ramekins on a baking sheet with a lip in case of any spills while baking.

After the dates and raisins have soaked, begin making the pudding. In a large bowl or standing electric mixer fitted with a paddle attachment, cream together the butter and brown sugar until it is light and fluffy. Scrape down the sides of the bowl. Beat in the eggs, one at a time, until they are fully incorporated, 2 to 4 minutes, then stir in the vanilla.

In small bowl, whisk together the flour, baking soda, baking powder, salt, cinnamon, ginger, cardamom, and nutmeg. Stir this into the wet ingredients until there are no visible, dry bits in the batter. Scrape down the sides and the bottom of the bowl to make sure that everything is combined well, about 4 minutes. Once the batter has come together, add the dates and raisins with the water and the instant espresso powder. Stir until the ingredients are fully combined, about 2 minutes.

(continued)

Makes 6 puddings

Sticky Toffee Pudding

1 cup (114 g) roughly chopped dates

¾ cup (108 g) raisins

1 cup (240 ml) boiling water

½ cup (116 g) salted butter, softened

1 cup (220 g) dark brown sugar, packed

4 large eggs

2 tsp (10 ml) vanilla extract

1¾ cups (219 g) all-purpose flour

1 tsp baking soda

½ tsp baking powder

½ tsp kosher salt

2 tsp (3 g) ground cinnamon

½ tsp ground ginger

½ tsp ground cardamom

¼ tsp ground nutmeg

2 tbsp (8 g) instant espresso powder

Brown Sugar—Poached Pears

6 firm, small, skinny pears (1.2 kg), such as Bosc or Concorde

2 cups (480 ml) water

1 cup (220 g) light brown sugar, packed

1 tsp vanilla extract

Place the cooled poached pears on a plate lined with a paper towel to drain. Fill the ramekins with the pudding batter about halfway up. Place the pears in the middle of the ramekins, and they should have batter covering about a quarter of the bottom of the pear. If there is any batter leftover, you may bake it separately.

Bake the puddings for 50 to 60 minutes, or until they are dark brown in color and a toothpick inserted into the puddings comes out clean.

While the puddings are baking, make the Toffee Sauce. In a small saucepan, combine the butter, whiskey, heavy cream, and brown sugar. Stir over medium-high heat until the butter melts and the sugar dissolves, bringing the sauce to a boil. Lower the heat to a simmer and cook, stirring occasionally, until the sauce thickens slightly, about 10 minutes. Remove the sauce from the heat and allow it cool slightly.

Once the puddings come out of the oven, drizzle them generously with the Toffee Sauce while they are still hot. Serve the puddings warm with any leftover Toffee Sauce on the side. To store, keep the puddings covered with plastic wrap in the refrigerator for 3 to 4 days.

Toffee Sauce

2 tbsp (29 g) salted butter

½ tbsp (8 ml) whiskey or apple cider

1 cup (240 ml) heavy cream

½ cup (110 g) light brown sugar, packed

Brie and Apple Crisp–Filled Baked Apples

As the crisp, autumnal air rustles through the apple orchard, it is easy to imagine the perfect treat to savor the season's bounty. Reminiscent of your favorite apple crisp, these baked apples are filled to the brim with a delightful mixture of warm cinnamon, tangy brie cheese, and a hearty oat crumble baked to perfection until they are soft. To complete this cozy and comforting dessert, serve with a generous scoop of homemade vanilla bean ice cream. It is the quintessential taste of fall, presented with all of the warmth and whimsy of a rustic cottage kitchen.

Preheat the oven to 400°F (204°C). Set aside a 9 x 9–inch (22 x 22–cm) baking dish.

Begin by making the Apple Crisp Filling. In a large bowl, mix together the oat flour, rolled oats, brown sugar, granulated sugar, rosemary, salt, cinnamon, and nutmeg until well blended. Cut the brie and butter into the oat mixture with a pastry blender or fork until the crumbles are about the size of a pea. Set this aside.

Peel and core four of the apples and chop them up into ½-inch (1.3-cm) chunks. In a large skillet, melt the butter over medium-high heat. Whisk in the brown sugar, cinnamon, and the apple chunks. Cook the apples, stirring occasionally, until the apples are softened and fork tender, 10 to 12 minutes. Remove the pan from the heat and set it aside.

Meanwhile, cut off the very tops of the remaining apples. With an apple corer or spoon, scoop out most of the inner flesh of the apples. Spoon the baked apple filling into the apples, filling them halfway full. Then, fill with the apple crisp filling until it begins to mound up on top of the apples.

Bake the apples in the preheated oven for 20 to 25 minutes, or until the inside is soft and bubbly, and the apples are tender. Top with a generous scoop of Vanilla Bean Ice Cream (page 178) and caramel sauce.

Store the apples covered in the refrigerator for 4 to 5 days.

Makes 4 apples

Apple Crisp Filling

¼ cup (32 g) oat flour

¼ cup (23 g) rolled oats

2 tbsp + 2 tsp (32 g) light brown sugar, packed

2 tbsp (25 g) granulated sugar

1 tsp fresh rosemary, chopped

¼ tsp kosher salt

½ tsp ground cinnamon

¼ tsp ground nutmeg

4 oz (113 g) brie, rind removed

2 tbsp (29 g) salted butter, cold and cut into cubes

Baked Apples

6 medium apples (1.5 kg), divided

6 tbsp (87 g) salted butter

½ cup (97 g) light brown sugar, packed

1 tsp ground cinnamon

Vanilla Bean Ice Cream, for serving (page 178)

Caramel sauce, for serving

Peach Bourbon Crisp with Vanilla Bean Ice Cream

I love the flavors of peaches, pecans, and bourbon mixed together in a perfect harmony. It is one of the best combinations for the late summer months. The velvety texture of peaches pairs seamlessly with the warm, smoky undertones of bourbon, a beloved American whisky made from corn. It is no wonder that these two summer essentials are ready for picking around the same time! Enjoy this lovely late summer delicacy made with your own locally grown produce.

First, make the Vanilla Bean Ice Cream. Set aside a 9 x 5–inch (23 x 13–cm) loaf pan.

In a large bowl, whip the heavy cream and sugar until it reaches stiff peaks, 5 to 6 minutes. Slowly drizzle in the sweetened condensed milk and vanilla, gently folding it together with the whipped cream. Alternately, if using a whole vanilla bean, slice it in half lengthwise and scrape out the seeds into the whipped cream and fold in.

Spread the cream into the loaf pan evenly. Cover the pan with plastic wrap and place the pan in the freezer until firm, about 3 hours.

Preheat the oven to 350°F (177°C). Grease a 9 x 13–inch (23 x 33–cm) pan and set this aside.

To make the Peach Bourbon Filling, in a large bowl combine the peach slices, sugar, cornstarch, lemon juice, lemon zest, bourbon, vanilla, and salt. Stir with a wooden spoon or spatula until everything is well coated, 2 to 4 minutes. Pour the filling into the prepared baking dish and set this aside.

Next, make the Cinnamon Oat Crumble. In a medium-sized bowl, combine the dark brown sugar, flour, rolled oats, pecans, cinnamon, nutmeg, and salt. With your fingers, blend in the butter, smashing it into pea-sized crumbles.

Spread the Cinnamon Oat Crumble over the Peach Bourbon Filling. Bake the crisp for 45 minutes, or until the crumble is golden brown and the filling is bubbly. Let the crisp cool for at least 15 to 20 minutes before serving with the Vanilla Bean Ice Cream.

To store, cover the crisp with foil and place in the refrigerator for 4 to 5 days. Store the ice cream in the freezer covered with a layer of plastic wrap, followed by a layer of foil. It should keep for 3 to 4 months.

Makes 1 (9 x 13–inch [23 x 33–cm]) pan

Vanilla Bean Ice Cream

2 cups (480 ml) heavy cream

½ cup (100 g) granulated sugar

1 (14-oz [392-g]) can sweetened condensed milk

1 tbsp (15 ml) vanilla bean paste or 1 whole vanilla bean

Peach Bourbon Filling

3 lbs (1.4 kg) peaches, peeled, pitted, and cut into ¼-inch (6-mm) slices

1 cup (200 g) granulated sugar

2 tbsp (16 g) cornstarch

1 tbsp (15 ml) fresh lemon juice

2 tsp (5 g) fresh lemon zest

1 tbsp (15 ml) bourbon or apple cider

½ tsp vanilla extract

Pinch of kosher salt

Cinnamon Oat Crumble

1 cup (194 g) dark brown sugar, packed

1 cup (125 g) all-purpose flour

½ cup (45 g) rolled oats

1 cup (100 g) chopped pecans

1 tsp ground cinnamon

¼ tsp ground nutmeg

¼ tsp kosher salt

¾ cup (174 g) salted butter, cold and cubed

Biscuit-Topped Blackberry Cobbler

While most modern cobblers have a cake-like topping, this cobbler is topped with soft, buttery biscuits—just like grandma used to make! This creates the cutest cobbler to serve with a big fluffy biscuit for every person, sprinkled with coarse sugar for a lovely little crunch. The blackberries are sweet and tart, a lovely ode to summer days.

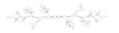

Preheat the oven to 425°F (218°C). Set aside a round 12-inch (30-cm) baking dish.

Begin by making the Buttermilk Biscuits. Set aside a large plate or small baking sheet. In a large bowl, whisk together the flour, baking powder, baking soda, and salt. Cut in the cold butter with a pastry blender or fork until the mixture resembles coarse crumbs about the size of a pea.

Stir in the buttermilk with a wooden spoon or silicone spatula. Bring the dough together with your hands until it is no longer dry and crumbly, about 2 minutes. On a lightly floured surface, fold the dough over itself about seven times to create layers in the dough.

Roll the dough out to about ½ inch (1.3 cm) thick and cut out the biscuits with a 3-inch (8-cm) round biscuit cutter. Be sure to cut straight down through the dough and do not twist the biscuit cutter. Place the cut biscuits on the large plate or baking sheet and refrigerate until ready to bake.

Next, make the Blackberry Filling. In a large bowl, gently mix together the blackberries, sugar, cornstarch, lemon juice, lemon zest, vanilla, and salt.

Pour the filling into the prepared baking dish. Arrange the cut biscuits over the top of the fruit filling. Then, brush the tops of the biscuits with the heavy cream and sprinkle them generously with the coarse sugar.

Bake the cobbler in the preheated oven for 20 to 25 minutes, or until the biscuits are golden brown and no longer doughy in the center, and the filling is bubbly. Let the cobbler rest for at least 15 to 20 minutes before serving. To store, keep the cobbler covered in the refrigerator for 4 to 5 days.

Makes 1 (12-inch [30-cm]) pan

Buttermilk Biscuits

2¼ cups (281 g) all-purpose flour

2 tsp (9 g) baking powder

½ tsp baking soda

½ tsp kosher salt

½ cup (116 g) salted butter, cold and cubed

1 cup (240 ml) cold buttermilk

2 tbsp (30 ml) heavy cream

¼ cup (48 g) coarse sugar, plus more for sprinkling

Blackberry Filling

3 cups (432 g) fresh blackberries

1 cup (200 g) granulated sugar

2 tbsp (16 g) cornstarch

1 tbsp (15 ml) fresh lemon juice

2 tsp (5 g) fresh lemon zest

1 tsp vanilla extract

Pinch of kosher salt

Personal Clementine Pavlovas

If you have not yet tried a pavlova, then you must give this recipe a try! While they seem intimidating at first, the process is really quite simple if you set aside some time in your day to give this incredibly soft and light dessert a try. Pavlovas are super light meringues, named after the famous Russian ballerina Anna Pavlova. They are cake-like with a crispy outer crust and magically soft filling inside. These personal pavlovas are flavored with orange extract and topped with the most delightful orange curd and whipped cream for a citrusy experience! Serve these at your next summer gathering with freshly squeezed lemonade.

Preheat the oven to 300°F (149°C) and line a large baking sheet with parchment paper.

In a large bowl, beat the egg whites with an electric handheld mixer or with a standing electric mixer fitted with a whisk attachment. Beat the whites on high speed until they become foamy and soft peaks form, or the tips of the peaks curl, 3 to 5 minutes.

Slowly begin to add the sugar, 1 tablespoon (15 g) at a time, waiting for the sugar to dissolve after each incorporation, 10 to 20 minutes, depending on the size of your sugar crystals and the speed of your mixer. If you are using fine granulated sugar, this can take up to 45 minutes. Continue to whip the meringue until stiff peaks form, or the peaks stand straight up and the meringue will cling to the bowl without falling if turned upside down.

Fold in the cornstarch, vinegar, and orange extract until it is no longer visible and the meringue is glossy, 1 to 2 minutes. If you would like your pavlovas to be a soft pink-orange, add 1 to 3 drops of pink or red food coloring or more until your desired color is reached.

Shape the pavlovas on the baking sheet lined with parchment paper. Pile four spoonfuls of meringue onto the parchment. Using a spatula, shape them to form little 4-inch (10-cm) circles, dragging the spatula up the sides so that it looks a bit like a cake. If you would like a fancier design, try piping the meringue with a cake tip instead!

Reduce the oven temperature to 250°F (121°C). Bake the pavlovas for 1 hour 15 minutes, or until dry and crisp to the touch. Turn off the oven and leave the pavlovas to cool inside of the oven for 3 hours, or until they are cooled completely. Try to avoid opening the oven.

(continued)

Makes about 4 pavlovas

Orange Pavlova

6 egg whites

1½ cups (300 g) caster or baker's sugar

3 tsp (13 g) cornstarch

1 tsp white distilled vinegar

1 tsp orange extract

Pink food coloring, optional

While the pavlovas are cooling, make the Blood Orange Curd and the Whipped Cream. To make the curd, whisk together the sugar, eggs, egg yolks, orange juice, and orange zest in a medium-sized double boiler over about 2 inches (5 cm) of simmering water. Whisk constantly to prevent the eggs from curdling or sticking to the pan. Continue to cook until the curd thickens and has the consistency of hollandaise sauce, about 10 minutes. Remove the pan from the heat and stir in the sliced butter. Pour the finished curd into a bowl or jar and cover it with plastic wrap that touches the surface of the curd. Allow it to cool to room temperature or chill to use later.

To make the Whipped Cream, beat the heavy cream and sugar on high speed with a wire whisk until it forms stiff peaks, or the peaks stand up on their own, 5 to 6 minutes.

Once the pavlovas have cooled, decorate them with a dollop of Whipped Cream and Blood Orange Curd. Add some fresh orange slices or whole clementines for a beautiful presentation!

To store the pavlovas, it is best to keep the ingredients separated. The pavlovas themselves should be left at room temperature in an airtight container for 3 to 4 days. The curd and Whipped Cream can be stored in the refrigerator in airtight containers for about 5 days.

Blood Orange Curd

1 cup (200 g) granulated sugar

2 large eggs

2 egg yolks

⅔ cup (160 ml) blood orange juice

2 tsp (5 g) orange zest

6 tbsp (87 g) salted butter, sliced

Whipped Cream

2 cups (480 ml) heavy cream

¼ cup (50 g) granulated sugar

Fresh clementines and blood oranges, for decoration

Acknowledgments

Thank you to my editor, Emily Archbold. You have been an absolute dream of an editor, and I am so thankful to have you! It is always so fun to talk about Cottagecore and dream about book concepts! Thank you for my endless supply of emails and questions, helping expand on new ideas, and being there to talk me through all of the little hiccups that come with writing a cookbook. I have appreciated all of the time that you have spent working on this book with me!

Thank you to Page Street Publishing for believing in me for a second time! This book was such a fun one to make, and I know that it will be happily held in the hands and hearts of readers who love a bit of rustic nostalgia for years to come. Thank you to Rosie Stewart for creating a beautiful book cover and design throughout this book. Thank you to Julia Fink. Thank you to the marketing team.

To my children, thank you for the hours spent waiting for your mother to finish her work. Thank you for being my little entertainers and for the endless supply of hugs and snuggles when the days felt long. Of course, thank you especially for being my best and most eager taste testers. With every bite or gasp of delight, my heart is so full! I love you three more than I can say.

To my husband, your support, understanding, and flexibility are things that I will forever be in awe of. You are my biggest fan, and I am yours. Thank you for all of the extra time spent taking care of our children while I baked and wrote, for talking me through all of my doubts and worries, and for loving me.

To my parents, you have always been there to tell me to keep going and that any of dreams were possible. I am so excited to share this book with you! Thank you, especially, to my mom for being my business partner and helping me to bring this book to life. Without your creative vision, ideas, and incredible illustrations, this book would not be the same product. I could not ask for a better team.

To my readers, I am forever indebted to you for helping make my career a possibility. You have been there from the beginning, and I am so incredibly thankful to be able to share this beautiful baking book with you all. I hope that I can continue to inspire you to bake beautiful and delicious creations at home in your kitchens! Your encouragement, praise, and love mean the world to me.

About the Author

Kayla Lobermeier is an author, blogger, recipe developer, content creator, homesteader, and owner of the brand Under A Tin Roof™. She works with her mother and business partner, Jill Haupt. She lives in rural Iowa with her husband, children, and parents on their multigenerational family farm. Under A Tin Roof™ is a cooking and lifestyle brand that focuses on sharing from scratch recipes inspired by cottage living, history, literature, and fantasy. Kayla has been sharing her food journey from growing to cooking to preserving with her readers for a decade. She is the author of *The Prairie Kitchen Cookbook* and has been featured in publications such as *Willow and Sage* magazine, *Where Women Cook, Heirloom Gardener, Folk* magazine, *In Her Garden, Beekman 1802 Almanac,* and *Gardenista*. She has taught cooking and gardening lessons throughout Kirkwood Community College and hosted farm-to-table suppers at her farm. You can usually find her sipping on a hot cup of coffee, reading up on the domestic lives of the Victorians, and snuggling with barn cats. Visit Kayla at underatinroof.com or Instagram, TikTok, and YouTube @underatinroof.

Index